BRAIN-COMPATIBLE CLASSROOMS

Robin Fogarty

SkyLight

PROFESSIONAL DEVELOPMENT

Arlington Heights, Illinois

Brain-Compatible Classrooms

Published by SkyLight Professional Development
2626 S. Clearbrook Dr., Arlington Heights, Illinois 60005-5310
Phone 800-348-4474, 847-290-6600
Fax 847-290-6609
info@skylightedu.com
http://www.skylightedu.com

Creative Director: Robin Fogarty
Managing Editor: Ela Aktay
Editor: Amy Kinsman
Book Designer: Bruce Leckie
Illustrator: David Stockman
Proofreader: Sue Schumer
Indexer: Dara Lee Howard

LCCCN 97-77395
ISBN 1-57517-044-2
Printed in the United States of America

2089-V
Item Number 1528
Z Y X W V U T S R Q P O N M L K J I H G F E
06 05 04 03 02 01 00 99   15 14 13 12 11 10 9 8 7 6 5

In loving memory
of my dad,
who knew just
how to grow dendrites.

CONTENTS

Acknowledgments . . . . *vii*

Preface . . . . *ix*

Introduction . . . . *xi*

CHAPTER 1 **Brain Research Base** 1

Physiology 2

Functioning 15

Nature vs Nurture (Heredity vs Environment) 23

Emotions and the Intellect 27

The Brain and the Mind 30

Theories of the Intellect 33

Memory, Learning, and the Brain 35

CHAPTER 2 **Defining Brain-Compatible Classrooms** 41

Implications for Schooling 42

The Framework of the Brain-Compatible Classroom 43

Definition of Brain-Compatible Classrooms 59

CHAPTER 3 **Setting the Climate for Thinking** 65

Brainwave #1 Emotions 68

Brainwave #2 Enriched Environment 94

CHAPTER 4 **Teaching the Skills of Thinking** 107

Brainwave #3 Types of Skills 110

Brainwave #4 Development of Skills 122

CHAPTER 5 **Structuring the Interaction with Thinking** . 135

Brainwave #5 Active Learning 138

Brainwave #6 Experiential Learning 168

CHAPTER 6 **Thinking about Thinking** 181

Brainwave #7 Reflection 184

Brainwave #8 Assessment 208

CHAPTER 7 **Teacher Evaluation** 217

Evaluation Tool 218

Setting the Climate: Teacher Evaluation＝Satisfactory 222

Teaching the Skills: Teacher Evaluation＝Good 223

Structuring Interaction: Teacher Evaluation＝Excellent 223

Teaching about Thinking: Teacher Evaluation＝Superior 224

Appendix A 227

Appendix B 229

Appendix C 231

Glossary 233

Reference List 239

Index 253

ACKNOWLEDGEMENTS

In my search for understanding about how the brain works and how class-rooms can become more brain-friendly, I want to acknowledge some leaders in the field: the pioneering work of Bob Sylwester and the caring advice he gave me, the generous sharing of Pat Wolfe, the wealth of ideas provided by Eric Jensen's books, and the bridge to learning provided by Geoffrey and Renate Caine's principles of brain research.

In my quest for quality, I want to thank my editing and design staff: Donna Ramirez for her skillful translation of both my handwriting and my disk, Dara Lee Howard for her insightful comments and drawings, Bruce Leckie for his ingenious layout and design, Dave Stockman for his daring cover art, and Amy Kinsman for her thoroughness and eye for consistencies.

In my journey toward lifelong learning, I want to mention three others: Brian for enduring endless hours of "brain tapes" as we traveled in the car, and Tim and Jeff for their unknowing contributions to my awareness of the brain and its inner workings.

I am indebted to all of the above.

ROBIN FOGARTY

PREFACE

If you are alive and well in the 90s, you know why this decade is known as The Decade of the Brain (Klein 1997). The exploration of our "universe within" is in full swing. From designer drugs such as Prozac and Zolof to catchy terms such as EQ and MRIs, the media is abuzz with the almost daily discoveries of how the brain functions and how that functioning can be monitored, improved, and even recreated. Popular magazines publish articles on brain-related stories and feature editions that devote whole issues to the mysteries of the human brain.

In fact, the nation and the world are fascinated by the findings in brain research. Such findings include the ability of people to go to sleep because melatonin simulates the dusklike qualities of light that trigger sleep; understanding why most males prefer not to ask for directions when lost, based on how male/female brains function; and learning about the "windows of opportunity" from birth to three years of age that facilitate the wiring and rewiring of the infant brain for learning language and moving about.

Brain references are popping up everywhere. People are aware of the dendrites in their brains and they talk about growing dendrites through problem-solving scenarios and, kiddingly, of killing dendrites with alcohol. The medical world is tapping into the research, and there are ground-breaking discoveries connecting brain chemistry and disease. Even educators are tuning in to brain-friendly strategies for learning.

With all this interest in the brain and the vast amount of information about the brain inundating the media, the need for an informative and practical book for teachers seems imminent. Thus, it is the purpose of this book, *Brain-Compatible Classrooms,* to bring the message of the brain research and its implications for the classroom to educators in a user-friendly format.

Yet, a word of caution is needed. The landscape of the brain research changes on almost a daily basis. With that in mind, be aware that information presented here is open to debate and alteration as new insights emerge. Take responsibility to read more on your own, concentrating on the resources cited within the last three years (see also Appendix C).

ROBIN FOGARTY
Chicago 1997

INTRODUCTION

Brain-Compatible Classrooms (BCC) is a book with a bit of a history. It is a reconceptualization of an earlier work titled, *Patterns for Thinking, Patterns for Transfer (Patterns)*. Based on a framework of four elements, *Patterns* presents a classroom model that advocates teaching *for, of, with,* and *about* thinking.

In essence, that same framework is restructured in *BCC*. Officially called the four-corner framework, this framework addresses the same four elements: setting the climate *for* thinking, teaching the skills *of* thinking, structuring the interaction *with* thinking, and thinking metacognitively *about* thinking. However, in *BCC,* the framework is really grounded in the emergent brain research, as well as in the sound pedagogical theory present in Patterns.

Chapter 1 of *BCC* presents the basics of the brain research in a brief discussion that is intended to provide an introductory awareness of the human brain and how it works. It begins with a thumbnail sketch of the physiology of the brain and the brain cell and proceeds to the functionality of how the brain/mind thinks, learns, and remembers. While this opening section serves to begin the conversation about the human brain, hopefully, it also serves as a bridge to further readings in the field of brain research.

Chapter 2 builds on this research base by applying the findings to the four-corner framework. Using a brilliant synthesis of the brain research, Renate and Geoffrey Caine have developed twelve principles that have compelling implications for the classroom. These twelve principles guide the creation of the framework and are summarized in the graphic on page xii.

In sum, the climate *for* thinking is governed by a safe climate and an enriched environment; skills *of* thinking encompass not only the types of skills but the developmental path of those skills; interaction *with* thinking targets active/experiential learning; and thinking *about* thinking highlights the reflection and assessment aspects of the high standards classroom.

Brainwaves in the Four-Corner Framework

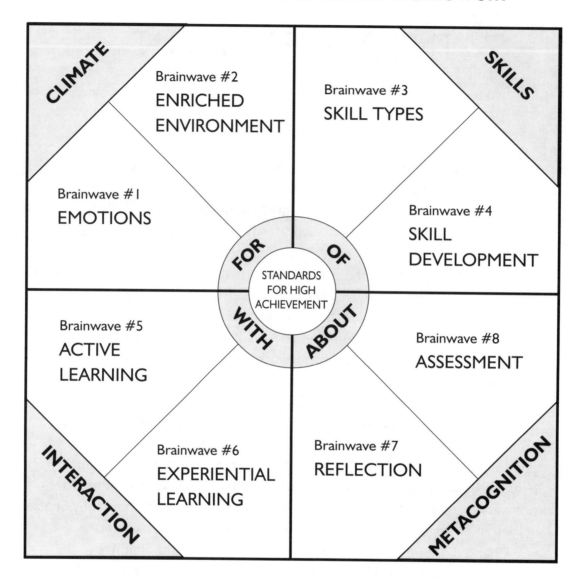

Thus, chapters 3, 4, 5, and 6 extrapolate the principles assigned to each of the four areas. Chapter 3 discusses extensive strategies and options for setting a peak learning climate, and chapter 4 exposes the essential life skills and the natural path from novice to expert to peak performance. Chapter 5 explores explicit strategies for active learners and the curricular models of authentic learning, while chapter 6 discusses the roles of reflective thinking and balanced assessments needed for learners to demonstrate deep understanding and relevant transfer.

SkyLight Training and Publishing, Inc.

Within each of these four chapters, certain brain-compatible elements appear. There are *brainwaves* (themes), *brainwise* (statements), *braindrops* (strategies), *brainworks* (activities), *brainstorms* (application), and *braindrain* (reflection). While the first two chapters provide the "soul" of the book, these four middle chapters form the "heart" of BCC. They offer a wealth of practical strategies and usable techniques for teachers in today's classrooms. Chapters 3, 4, 5, and 6 put life to the theory and are intended to guide immediate application.

In the final chapter, chapter 7, the four-corner framework is viewed from the perspective of different levels of teaching skill. Each of the four corners of the framework is considered in the form of a taxonomy of teaching. Skill in all four arenas provides the ultimate model for effective teaching and the taxonomy is presented for readers to scrutinize and review.

The book is designed as a comprehensive treatment of today's high-challenge classroom and the intricate complexities that comprise that classroom. It is meant to provide a holistic model that is useful for teachers to use in designing their own classrooms. Thus, readers may choose to devour the whole picture, page by page, chapter by chapter, as designed; or, they may prefer to sample bite-size pieces at a more leisurely pace. In either case, there are certain advantages and disadvantages.

In approaching *BCC* as a complete framework for teaching and learning, the reader sees the big picture and the interrelationships among the four areas. The four-corner framework literally affords the reader a look at how it all fits together. On the other hand, by attacking the entire text as one piece, the reader may not have the luxury of immersion in content of specific interest. For example, there may be compelling ideas in the first chapter on the human brain that one wants to pursue before moving on to the practical implications of that information.

If, from the other perspective, the reader delves into separate sections of personal relevance, the content may invite further investigation and in-depth exploration. Yet, with the deep-dive approach, the framework may never emerge as a unifying thread. It is so easy to get lost within one section, and miss the moment to bridge the various elements of *BCC* into a meaningful whole.

Still, it seems in keeping with the spirit of the book to trust the inquiring mind of the reader and advocate both approaches, whole to part and part to whole, as equally rewarding. After all, learning is that personal and each reader will do what he or she does naturally, regardless of the wishes or intent of the author. Ultimately, of course, the purpose of BCC is to inspire teachers in the architecture of their own uniquely designed brain-compatible classrooms. So off you go...read on.

CHAPTER 1

BRAIN RESEARCH BASE

Minds differ still more than faces.
—Voltaire

CHAPTER 1

BRAIN RESEARCH BASE

Physiology

She's a brain! You're a numskull! That's a harebrained idea! Have you lost your mind? Are you out of your mind? Put on your thinking cap. Use your noodle. I'm having a brain drain. Use your gray matter. These are just some of the remarks one hears in everyday references to the brain and the mind. In fact, these sayings offer concrete evidence for the common understandings people have, and have had for some time, about the brain. Yet, with the recent avalanche of information available through brain imaging technologies about cognitive functioning, interest in the brain seems to be increasing. As brain research explodes in what is known as The Decade of the Brain (Klein 1997), parents, teachers, educators, and students themselves have become intrigued with the emergent knowledge of how their brains remember and learn.

What Are the Facts About the Brain?

Scientists have discovered several facts about the 100 billion nerve cells, called neurons, that make up the organ called the human brain. This unique organ is located in the head and is protected by the cranium, or skull. The average brain weighs approximately three pounds, is about the size of a cantaloupe split in half, appears wrinkled like a walnut, and feels somewhat like an avocado that has ripened.

While the brain accounts for only 2 percent of a person's body weight, it uses 20 percent of the energy in the body and generates twenty-five watts of power (enough energy to illuminate a light bulb) when a person is awake. Messages travel within the brain through neural connections at speeds up to 250 miles per hour, and several billion bits of information pass though your brain each and every second of your life.

The study of the brain is considered biology, while the study of the mind is considered psychology. Both the neurobiological evidence and the cognitive-psychological findings offer scientists and researchers a better understanding of the brain and the mind and of their inner workings. While most educators are interested in how the mind works and what they can do to enhance learning, knowing how the brain itself works is an important prerequisite in shaping what is referred to here as brain-compatible classrooms; classrooms in which the teaching/learning process is structured to parallel the ways the brain obtains and retains information.

To begin, focus on the brain and what is known about this amazing organ: Read the following statements in Figure 1.1 and try to agree or disagree with them in terms of your first thought or intuition.

How Has the Brain Evolved?

MacLean's triune brain theory (Hart 1983) is an early model of the brain that tracks a theory of evolutionary development to the modern human brain. This model provides a simple, easily understood concept of the human brain; therefore, it is presented here. Be warned that this model is suspect in current literature (LeDoux 1996) because of its simplicity and its possible misrepresentations of the human brain as it is known today. However, for the purpose of this book, the simplistic nature gives teachers a glimpse as to how the brain is structured. If readers need a more detailed explanation of the brain, there are primary sources listed in Appendix C. According to MacLean's theory, three separate and distinct brains comprise the triune brain: the reptilian, the paleomammalian, and the neomammalian (see Figure 1.2). As each brain evolved, the older brain was retained for its specific functions, and the newer brain simply formed around the older one.

In this early model, it is the belief that the ancestral brain developed about 500 million years ago. It is referred to as the reptilian brain, or the lower or hind brain. The reptilian brain is located in the brain stem, which controls physical responses. This stem is really an extension of the spinal cord, and it is about as thick as the middle finger on a person's hand (Wolfe 1996a). The swelling on the stem is called the medulla oblongata. The medulla oblongata governs survival, sustenance, safety, and sex. It is the main controller of heartbeat and breathing, and other instictual reflexes including snoring, coughing, sneezing, and even digesting. It regulates instincts including the reflexive activities of fight or flight. As one well-known writer on brain research says, this is the brain that automatically decides and responds to the

BRAIN QUIZ*

1. The brain is like a sieve.

2. Noodle, noggin, gray matter, and thinking cap refer to the brain.

3. One is born with a certain number of dendrites that doesn't change.

4. Human brains are getting bigger.

5. The brain and the mind are one.

6. Use it or lose it! applies to our brains.

7. Your brain power is inherited.

8. Brains are as individual as fingerprints.

9. We have an old brain and a new brain.

10. Our brains are plastic.

11. Alcohol actually kills brain cells.

12. Reasoning usually rules over emotions.

13. The brain rewires itself.

14. Male and female brains are quite different.

15. The mind resides inside the brain.

16. The brain is not really much like a computer.

17. The brain is a jungle ecosystem.

18. You can stop thinking on signal.

19. That added a wrinkle to my brain, means your brain just aged.

20. "Brain rain" is caused by brainstorms.

* Answers appear on page 6 in Figure 1.1a.

Figure 1.1

SkyLight Training and Publishing, Inc.

The Triune Brain: An Early Model of the Brain

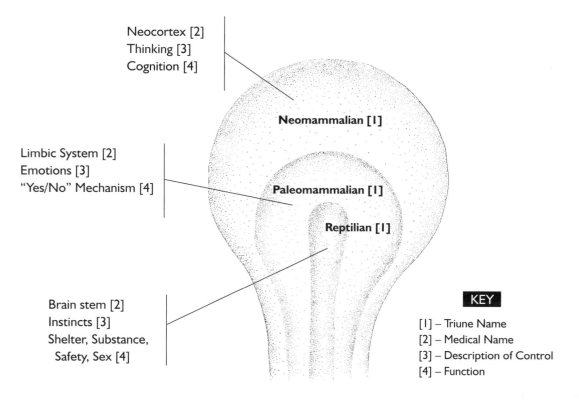

Neocortex [2]
Thinking [3]
Cognition [4]

Neomammalian [1]

Limbic System [2]
Emotions [3]
"Yes/No" Mechanism [4]

Paleomammalian [1]

Reptilian [1]

Brain stem [2]
Instincts [3]
Shelter, Substance,
Safety, Sex [4]

KEY

[1] – Triune Name
[2] – Medical Name
[3] – Description of Control
[4] – Function

Figure 1.2

questions Do I eat it? Fight it? Run away from it? Or mate with it? (Sylwester 1996).

The second brain delineated in MacLean's model is the paleomammalian brain, or the limbic system, which MacLean argues evolved around 250 million years ago. This brain responds through its emotional system to all sensory input. It is located in the cerebellum, or middle brain, and surrounds the brain stem like a donut. The paleomammalian brain controls the sensory input of taste and smell, memory storage, motor muscles, and movement. It controls the ability to automate the skills of riding a bike, knitting, or keyboarding. This limbic system contains the thalamus (senses), hypothalamus (emotions, body temperature, hunger, thirst, and sex drive), the pituitary gland (hormones for energy), the pinal gland (rate of body growth), the amygdala (trigger for anger) and the hippocampus (new memories). In addi-

ANSWERS TO BRAIN QUIZ

1. **T** (Sousa—In the early stages of processing, the brain drops data it doesn't need or think it will use.)

2. **T** (Can you add other terms that describe the muscle between your ears?)

3. **F** (Diamond—People can grow dendrites by stimulation of a rich environment.)

4. **T** (Barrett—People's brains are 1/2 lb more than their great grandparents' brains.)

5. **T** (Sylwester—the brain)

6. **T** (Margulies—If the brain is not used, dendrites don't grow.)

7. **F** (Margulies—nature vs nurture)

8. **T** (Jensen—Each brain is unique.)

9. **T** (MacLean—triune brain theory)

10. **T** (Margulies—They change and grow with experiences.)

11. **T** (Margulies—Alcohol kills cells; Wolfe—Fetal Alcohol Syndrome)

12. **F** (Margulies—Emotions [limbic system] can hijack thinking.

13. **T** (Kotulak—The brain rewires to threats, etc.)

14. **T** (Jensen—They have different length and density of nerve cells and strands.)

15. **T** (Barrett—The brain is biology; the mind is psychology.)

16. **T** (Sylwester)

17. **T** (Edleman in Sylwester—Brain is most like jungle ecosystem in its random, interconnected growth patterns.)

18. **F** (Sylwester—Your brain processes even when asleep.)

19. **F** (Moye—An old saying about "getting a new idea.")

20. **T** (Fogarty—Brain rain is just another way of saying brainstorm of ideas.

Figure 1.1a

tion, the reticular activating system (RAS) acts as a master switch that alerts the brain to incoming information and to the urgency or lack of urgency in the message.

The limbic system is often referred to as the guardian at the gate—the guardian of emotions at the gate of the intellect. Emotions are seen as the gateway to the thinking mind. If the emotional guard is up, very little cognitive reasoning is likely to occur. The emotions rule over reason, and thinking is often blurred when emotions are high. This is illustrated in a situation in which a person is so mad that he or she cannot think.

This brain regulates feelings of happiness, joy, sorrow, sadness, grief, jealousy, greed, and hate. The brain responds emotionally to stimuli and, in states of great threat, is the default system that activates first. MacLean's early theory suggests the limbic system is the center of emotions and Hart (1983) presents a concept of "downshifting" to this emotional brain in the face of threat. Yet, more current theory suggests that the emotional brain alerts the body that threat is realized subconsciously in the emotional state before it is understood in the conscious rational state.

The third brain, labeled the neomammalian by MacLean, is known as the thinking brain. It is located in the cerebrum and considered the center of academic thought and cognitive learning. It forms the top layer of the triune brain model and is referred to as the forebrain, upper brain, or new brain. While not represented as such in the simplified drawing, the neocortex, or "bark," actually consists of 85 percent of the total brain. As the new brain adapted, evolved, and grew larger, the skull did not grow as quickly; there-fore, the cerebrum, which is as thick as a tongue depressor, is full of convolu-tions, and its size is equivalent to the size of an open newspaper. Known as the thinking cap, this brain handles the cognitive functions of the brain and the mind. It predicts, classifies, judges, infers, reasons, puzzles, wonders, creates, reflects, and makes sense of things. This is the brain that sets humans apart from other species of animals. The neocortex, as it has evolved in the human brain, leads to the idea of a brain and a mind. The brain does not think but the mind does.

The triune brain model (see Figure 1.3) is truly an over-simplification of the human brain, but it does allow a look at the various functions the brain performs. In addition, it is critical to understand that the brain adapted to its changing environmental needs over time and that the various parts are intri-

Triune Brain Model: An Early Model

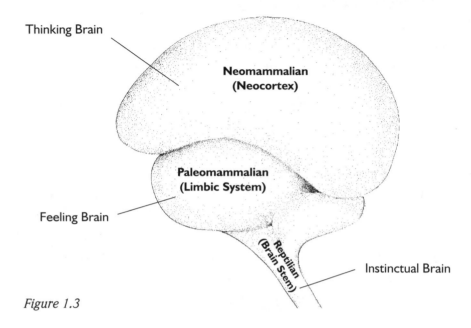

Thinking Brain

**Neomammalian
(Neocortex)**

**Paleomammalian
(Limbic System)**

Feeling Brain

**Reptilian
(Brain Stem)**

Instinctual Brain

Figure 1.3

cately related and work together as they are in constant communication with each other.

In fact, in current literature, the triune model is thought to be a misrepresentation of the human brain for a number of reasons. In contemporary thinking about a model for the brain, the illustration needs to emphasize that the neocortex is much larger than any other part of the brain. The model needs to clarify that the limbic system is much smaller than it appears in the triune brain model and is not the sole "seat of emotions" but, rather, that emotions are probably organized in multiple ways throughout the brain—similar to the emerging concept of multiple intelligences. However, the triune brain model, with all its shortcomings, does help illuminate the subsequent views of the brain: top/bottom, front/back, left/right.

Three Views of the Brain

A further look at the brain, apart from MacLean's triune brain theory, reveals not only a top/bottom dichotomy and frontal/hind lobes but also left and right hemispheres, or bilateralization. By examining each of these views, additional features of the human brain can be illuminated.

By making a fist with both hands and touching the knuckles of one hand to the knuckles of the other hand, a model of the general shape of the brain results (see Figure 1.4). Interestingly, there appears to be no correlation between the size of the brain and intelligence.

Fists Simulating the Brain

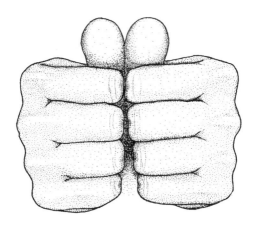

Figure 1.4

TOP/BOTTOM

The top/bottom dichotomy somewhat parallels MacLean's triune brain theory. Figure 1.5 depicts the top to bottom view of the brain. The top, or neocortex, is the outer most layer of the brain. Cortex, which means bark, comprises four-fifths of the entire organ known as the brain (Sylwester 1995). This top layer is often referred to as the thinking brain because all higher level cognitive functions happen in this folded section of the brain.

Moving from the top layer down, the middle section of the brain, or the limbic system, controls the emotions. It is the feeling brain, and it signals the body to receive or express emotions, to accept or reject possibilities. It is in constant conversation with the thinking brain above it and the ancestral brain beneath it.

Finally, at the bottom layer of the brain, or the brain stem, is the reptilian or instinctual brain, which governs our survival mechanisms. This is the part of the brain that alerts the body to the fight or flight syndrome and to territorial concerns and needs for survival. It is probably the oldest part of the brain, evolving from the reptilian era as the brain adapted to its environmental needs in a Darwinian way.

Top to Bottom

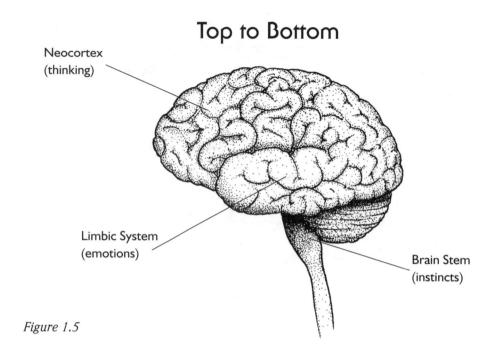

Neocortex
(thinking)

Limbic System
(emotions)

Brain Stem
(instincts)

Figure 1.5

FRONT/BACK

According to Aleksander Luria (in Rico 1991), the frontal and hind lobes of the brain appear to sense temporal dimensions as well as spatial conceptual organization. This view of the brain from front to back is shown in Figure 1.6. The frontal lobe relates to the future. It is involved in planning, in making decisions, and in identifying one's sense of self. This frontal lobe is also the area where rehearsal takes place and where the brain allows risk taking (Sylwester 1995). It gives foresight (Rico 1991) into situations. It is also the part concerned with problem solving and critical thinking. It helps make judgments, classify general categories, and estimate.

The middle section, moving from front to back, is most sensitive to stimuli in the present. It is the center of sensory/motor input.

The hind brain, situated furthest back, focuses on the past and is where memory is processed. In this area, the temporal lobes process hearing, and the occipital lobes process vision. This part of the brain collects and retrieves information. It contains the parietal lobe that processes touch.

LEFT/RIGHT

Viewed from above, the brain is divided into right and left hemispheres along a line running from the nose directly back (see Figure 1.7). The two sides are

Front to Back

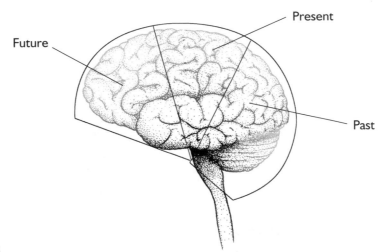

Figure 1.6

connected by the corpus callosum, which comprises a dense band of more than 200 million axons and acts as a bridge or pathway that interconnects the intricate hemispheric system.

Thus, while lateralization (differentiation of tasks) does occur, the hemispheres are in constant communication with each other through the synchronization of the corpus callosum. Yet, a closer look at the hemispheres reveals just how complex the tailoring of tasks for each side really is. More specifically, numerous researchers document this lateralization in terms of different ways of processing related information, helping the brain combine all the information to produce a more complete mental experience.

For example, the left side of the brain is thought to process language-related ideas, reasoned judgments, and logical sequencing (Hart 1983), to provide literal interpretations (Barrett 1992), to give structure and order to thoughts (Jensen 1996a), to bring critical analysis to an idea (Sylwester 1995), to split and classify ideas (Rico 1991), as well as to deal with numbers and the calculations of arithmetic (Sousa 1995). While this is generally true in most right handed people, it is true for fewer left handed people. In fact, some people have mirror brains, where everything is reversed and some have quite mixed up brains.

In contrast, the right side of the brain seems to process spatial information and visual patterns (Hart 1983), to scan images, to utilize intuition, and

12

Left to Right

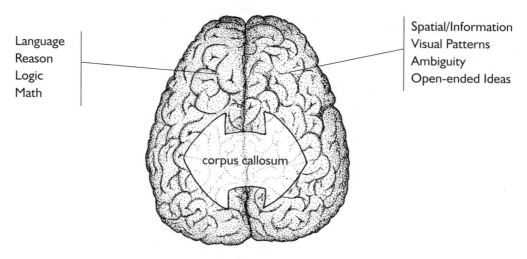

Language
Reason
Logic
Math

Spatial/Information
Visual Patterns
Ambiguity
Open-ended Ideas

corpus callosum

Figure 1.7

to take in data simultaneously (Barrett 1992). In addition, the right side of the brain deals with spontaneous, random, and open-ended ideas (Jensen 1996a), as well as novel situations, paradox, and ambiguity (Rico 1991). This is the part of the brain that relates information; reads maps, graphs, and cartoons (Sylwester 1995); and is able to "go with the flow" (Jensen 1996c).

While hemisphericity in brain research on how the brain works made an early debut (Sperry 1968), current thinking is cautious to apply the left/right brain concept too rigorously or too exclusively. Tempered with the overall understanding of synchronization of the two hemispheres, a more reasoned and generally accepted view of the bilateralization of brain processing is preferred.

Topography of the Brain

To provide a "big picture" look at the brain, Figure 1.8 depicts a general geography of the brain. While this is a grossly simplified version of the geography of the human brain, it does represent major areas and the accompanying function of those areas.

Geography of the Brain

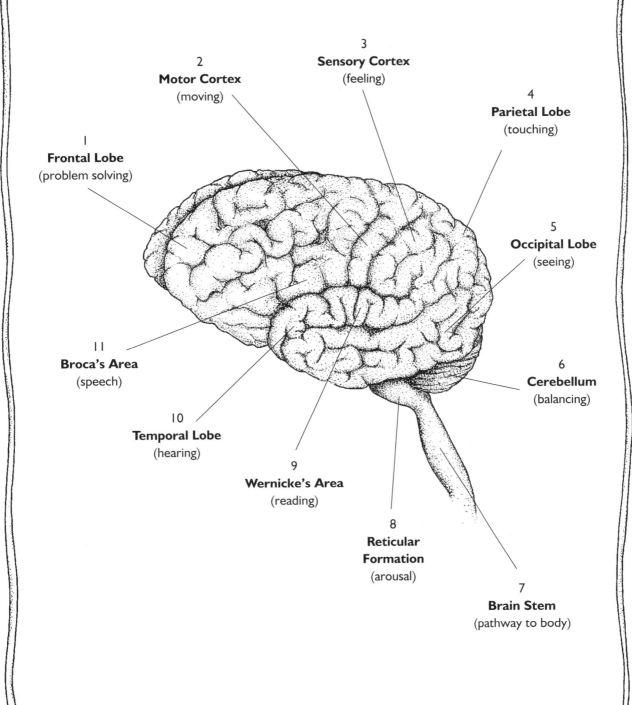

3
Sensory Cortex
(feeling)

2
Motor Cortex
(moving)

4
Parietal Lobe
(touching)

1
Frontal Lobe
(problem solving)

5
Occipital Lobe
(seeing)

11
Broca's Area
(speech)

6
Cerebellum
(balancing)

10
Temporal Lobe
(hearing)

9
Wernicke's Area
(reading)

8
**Reticular
Formation**
(arousal)

7
Brain Stem
(pathway to body)

Figure 1.8

Moving around the drawing (see Figure 1.8) from position 1 to position 11, the areas represented are

1. The frontal lobe is located in the neocortex or cerebrum. This region is future-oriented and thinks creatively and analytically in a problem-solving mode. It also takes part in the complex behaviors called personality.

2. The motor cortex governs movement and the overall motor control. It is seen as one of two distinctive channels in the neocortex.

3. The sensory cortex involves the sensory input and appears as the second channel in the neocortex, near the motor cortex region.

4. The parietal lobe, located at the top of the brain, is often associated with touch and the sense of feeling received from all over the skin. It senses hot and cold, hard and soft, and degrees of pain. It also senses taste and smell.

5. The occipital lobe, located in the hind brain rules over vision and the ability to see and observe. It works out shapes, colors, and movements and is the site of the "mind's eye."

6. The cerebellum, part of the hind brain, is the center of balance for the human body. It coordinates movement as it monitors impulses from nerve endings in the muscles.

7. The brain stem, located at the back of the brain and extending to the spinal column, is the brain path to the body. It is the center for sensory reception and monitors vital bodily functions such as heartbeat, breathing, and digestion.

8. The reticular formation located on the brain stem is the trigger for arousal. It integrates the sensory information into a general level of attention. It acts as a chemical net that opens and closes to the incoming information flow.

9. Wernicke's area is considered the center of reading in the language region of the neocortex.

10. The temporal lobe in the neocortex, located above and behind the ears, is the center for hearing and auditory impact. It receives auditory signals and identifies sounds by comparing them with sound patterns in the memory banks.

11. Broca's Area is the center for speech in the neocortex and relates to other language areas of writing and reading.

Functioning

Before the in-depth discussion describing how the brain actually functions, it seems appropriate to talk a bit about how researchers know what they know about the workings of the brain and what has caused the recent avalanche of ideas about the brain in what is known as The Decade of the Brain (Klein 1997).

How We Know What We Know

The major breakthrough in neurobiological research is attributed to advanced brain imaging techniques. A quick reference to the various brain imaging methods reveals a concentration on three elements of brain function and neural organization: the chemical composition of cells and neurotransmitters (CAT, MRI), the electrical transmission of information along the neural pathways (EEG, SQUID, BEAM), and the distribution of blood during brain activity (PET). This array of acronyms: CAT, MRI, EEG, SQUID, BEAM, and PET comprise the brain imaging techniques (see Figure 1.9).

Together, these imaging techniques confirm earlier theories and revelations about how the brain functions and where particular functions occur. The explosion of information about the brain is unprecedented.

How the Brain Works

To fully understand how the brain works, it seems best to begin by identifying the parts of the brain cell: neuron, axon, dendrite, synapse, neurotransmitter, electrical impulse, chemical signal, glial cell, myelin, and neural network, or pathway (see Figure 1.10). The brain is mostly composed of microscopic nerve cells called neurons, sometimes referred to as "gray matter" (Barrett 1992). Sylwester (1995) describes the human brain as being composed of neurons and glial cells. Glia means glue, and these glial cells are indeed an important part of the architecture of the brain. They form part of a blood barrier to protect the brain from dangerous molecules that travel in the bloodstream. Glial cells also form a layer of insulation (myelin) around nerve fibers, which strengthens and increases the neural messages.

BRAIN IMAGING TECHNIQUES: A GLOSSARY OF TERMS

CAT: Computerized Axial Tomography

The CAT scan produces anatomical views of the brain that show three-dimensional graphical images of the density of tissue, such as bone and tumors. Multiple x-ray pictures can show depth of field and cross-sectional views on a computer monitor (Sylwester 1995; Parker 1995).

MRI: Magnetic Resonance Imaging

Unlike the CAT scan, the MRI focuses on soft tissue and provides a reverse image by responding to chemical differences in composition. New MRI techniques work so fast that researchers can monitor brain activity while a cognitive activity is happening (Barrett 1992; Sylwester 1995).

EEG: Electroencephalogram

Used for over fifty years, the EEG process reports patterns in electrical transmissions within an active brain. These patterns are recorded as a squiggly line graph on a roll of paper. Obtaining accurate readings and interpretations and translating a score is often difficult (Sylwester 1995; Herrmann 1995; Parker 1995; Davis, 1997; Solso 1997).

SQUID: Superconductivity Quantum Interference Device

This technique picks up small magnetic fields caused by the electrical current of firing neurons to pinpoint the exact source of brain activity. This identifies a more exact source of electrical activity (Sylwester 1995; Barrett 1992).

BEAM: Brain Electrical Activity Mapping

This is a machine that records electrical activity in more precisely defined areas and uses color to represent positive and negative locations in the cerebral cortex (Sylwester 1995).

PET: Positron Emission Tomography

The PET uses radioactive glucose to monitor the blood flow through the brain as various areas are activated. This reveals information about how and where an experience is processed in the brain (Sylwester 1995; Barrett 1992).

Figure 1.9

SkyLight Training and Publishing, Inc.

THE BRAIN CELL:
A GLOSSARY OF TERMS

NEURON: nerve cell that comprises gray and white matter in the brain

AXON: long fibers that send electrical impulses and release neuro-transmitters

DENDRITE: short branching that receives the chemical transmitters

SYNAPSE: small gap between neurons through which neurotransmitters move

NEUROTRANSMITTER: chemical molecule that travels within and between brain cells

ELECTRICAL IMPULSE: the nerve messages received and sent out by the neurons

CHEMICAL SIGNAL: a message carried from neuron to neuron; chemical molecules called neurotransmitters traveling across synapses

GLIAL CELL: cells that split and duplicate to act as glue to strengthen brain cells

MYELIN: coating on the axon that serves as an insulator and speeds up transmission for outgoing messages

NEURAL NETWORK: a set of connected neurons that form a strengthened path that cases and speeds the passage of the neuron transmitters

Figure 1.10

SkyLight Training and Publishing, Inc.

The neuron can be compared to a drawing of a human arm, hand, and fingers, as shown in Figure 1.11. The cell body is like the hand, the axon is the arm (acting as a conductor that carries the impulse to the next cell), and the fingers form the equivalent of the dendrites (the receptors of the impulse) (Sylwester 1995).

Physical Model of a Neuron

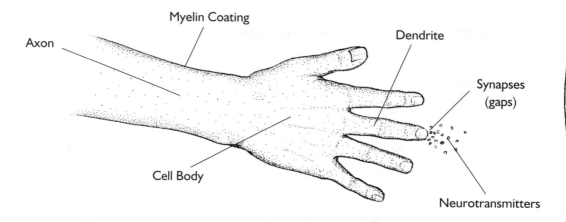

Figure 1.11

When the neuron receives a message from the senses, muscles, or other neurons, it is received as an electrical impulse. This impulse is processed inside the cell, then it is sent out to other neurons by way of the axons (Wolfe 1996b). Traveling at speeds of 100 miles per hour, the impulse travels on the outside of the axon. When the electrical impulse reaches the end of the axon, near the dendrite branches, chemical neurotransmitters are released into the synapse and are received by the dendrite (Sylwester 1995). These synapses allow neurons to communicate with each other. Thus, the reaction along the axon is electrical, while the reaction between the cells is chemical (Parker 1995). This process results in electrochemical interactions.

Synaptic Connection

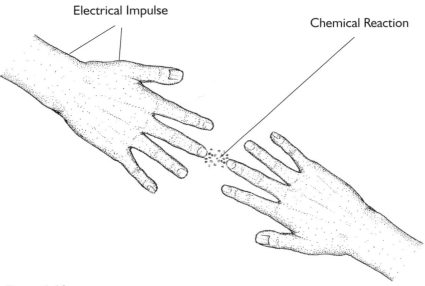

Electrical Impulse

Chemical Reaction

Figure 1.12

The synaptic connection, using the hand metaphor, is shown in Figure 1.12 to illustrate how neurons communicate.

Neuron Communication

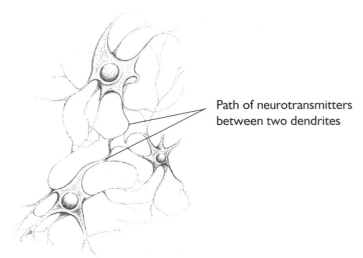

Path of neurotransmitters between two dendrites

Figure 1.13

A more scientific look at the synaptic connection highlights the strength of the dendrites (see Figure 1.13).

Synapse

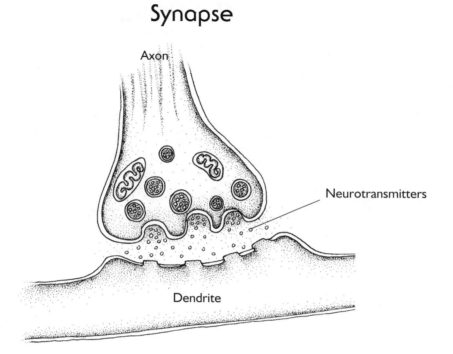

Axon

Neurotransmitters

Dendrite

Figure 1.14

Still a closer look at the synaptic connection reveals the intricate path of the neurotransmitters (see Figure 1.14).

Chemical Messengers Called Neurotransmitters

Neurotransmitters are the chemical messengers that communicate between neurons at the synapse, or the narrow gap between the axon and the dendrite. These chemical neurotransmitters are released as the electrical neural impulse is passed from one neuron to another.

Scientists have identified more that fifty neurotransmitters, but for the sake of this introductory chapter on the brain, only a few are defined in this text. They are grouped into three categories: amino acids, monoamines, and peptides (see Figure 1.15).

Amino acids are the principle neurotransmitters. They carry excitatory or inhibitory messages. Monoamines determine whether the message sent is excitatory or inhibitory. Peptides or classical neurotransmitter effect complex behavior patterns such as pain and pleasure.

NEUROTRANSMITTERS:
A GLOSSARY OF TERMS

Amino Acids

SIMPLE GLUTAMATE: excitatory neurotransmitter (vision, learning, and memory)

GABA OR GLYCINE: inhibitory neurotransmitter (reduces anxiety and relaxes muscles)

Monoamines Modified

DOPAMINE: regulates complex emotional behaviors and conscious movements

SEROTONIN: regulates body temperature, sensory perception, and the onset of sleep

NOREPINEPHRINE: regulates arousal, activation, fight or flight

Peptides Complex

ENDORPHIN: reduces pain, enhances euphoria

VASOPRESSIN: water retention, blood pressure, memory

*For more detailed listings and definitions of these terms, refer to *A Celebration of Neurons,* by Robert Sylwester.

Figure 1.15

The billions of nerve cells connect, in this way, to each other in billions of combinations, forming trillions of pathways for nerve signals to follow. What results is referred to as dendritic growth, and the dendrites continue to grow and interconnect throughout a lifetime. These brain connections or neural pathways are wired and rewired constantly, continually, and incessantly as stimuli are processed by the brain (see Figure 1.16). The possible combinations are mind-boggling as the permutations expand.

Diagram of Growing Dendrites

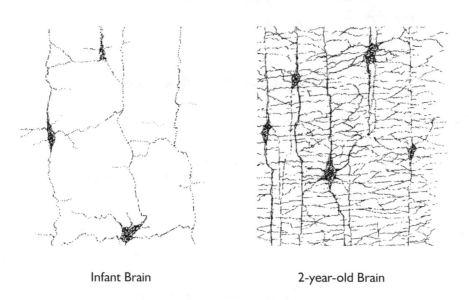

Infant Brain   2-year-old Brain

Figure 1.16

Documented in Potter and Orfali (1993), an additional commentary on dendritic growth is the age old axiom Use it or lose it! Just as stimulation fosters the growth of dendrites, the lack of stimuli causes the existing connection to weaken and even to disappear. While "pruning" (the natural weeding of old, unused dendritic connections, or neural pathways) is a natural process in growing dendrites, the concept of losing brain capacity refers to dramatic situations in which there is almost a total lack of stimulation for brain growth (Wolfe 1996a).

Nature vs Nurture (Heredity vs Environment)

The controversy about the role of heredity vs the role of environment or the nature vs nurture dilemma rages on. Evidence abounds that the role of environment is probably much more critical to the development of the brain function than was previously believed. Although most researchers agree that heredity plays a major role in determining the potential for brain growth and cognitive development, there is overwhelming evidence to suggest that an enriched environment stimulates brain activity and subsequent development of higher functioning intellects (Diamond 1988).

The ability of the brain to adapt to its environment by laying down essential neural connections is referred to as neural plasticity. This concept is seen as a result of experience. When researchers say that intelligence is a function of experience, they literally mean that experiences do cause continual rewiring of the neural pathways within the brain (Sylwester 1995).

Although a previously held belief that the brain is a "blank slate" to be filled by experience is too radical, the idea that "it's in the genes" in terms of smart or not smart, is also, too drastic. Most likely, a reasoned voice would argue that a person's potential is governed by both natural genetic makeup and relevant environmental factors (Healy 1990).

Enriched Environments

An enriched environment has a variety of rich sensory and language experiences that literally stimulate a profusion of dendritic growth. The more dendrites one grows, the more pathways or connections one makes and, in turn, the more capacity one has for establishing patterns and seeing the interrelatedness between ideas. This leads to the "chunking of information" so that all the information is remembered as a single item (Wolfe 1996b). (Patterning and chunking are discussed in detail later in this chapter.)

More specifically, Healy (1994) speaks of enriched environments that involve basic considerations such as safety and regular contact with others. Enriched environments also include appropriate play materials such as blocks, clay, paints, building sets; creative playthings that require intense, active learning; restricted television viewing time; and opportunities for daily outings. Wolfe (1994) makes a key point in her warning that no matter how well planned, how interesting, or how colorful or relevant the experience, if the child does not interact with that rich environment, little learning takes place and the dendrites are not stimulated to grow.

Jensen (1996c) includes a number of criteria in his discussion of enriched environments: room arrangement; formal and informal seating arrangements; low lighting; more water (eight to fifteen glasses a day); clean air; real world and multisensory experiences; multimodel experiences; challenging, novel, and rich activities; greater time flexibility (two hour blocks); and opportunities for making choices.

Sylwester (1996) explains that because "neurons thrive only in an environment that stimulates them to receive, store, and transmit information, the challenge to educators is simple: define, create, and maintain an emotionally and intellectually stimulating environment and curriculum" (pp. 129–130).

Intelligence as a Function of Experience

In addition to and embedded in the idea of an enriched environment is the range of experiences students are exposed to both in school and outside of school. These experiences result from an extension of the enriched home or classroom environment and reach out into the community and the world beyond. These experiences imprint on the mind and stimulate brain growth and neural connections, just as the more formally planned experiences in the classroom do.

For example, a fishing trip with grandpa, a walk along the wooded path, playing in the tree house, going to the museum, and even watching the clouds go by are the types of sensory experiences that kids need to interact with. Conversations with elders, laughing and teasing with siblings, or talking with friends are the kinds of language experiences that complement the parent/teacher dialogues and stimulate brain activity. Intelligence is truly a function of experience, so it is critical that whatever gifts nature endowed us with are further enhanced and stimulated by rich and fertile experiences.

Windows of Opportunity

Closely connected to the concept of the role of nature vs the role of nurture and the accompanying concept of neural plasticity is the idea often referred to as windows of opportunity. Another way to think about these windows of opportunity is to think of them as critical periods in which the plasticity of the brain is at its peak for learning in a particular area.

In other words, there seems to be optimal times for the neural pathways to develop as larger and heavier cortical tissue, which means that future connections are made more frequently and more easily. These sturdy connections are sometimes referred to as "hardwiring" (Healy 1994) in the brain. One example of this is binocular vision (the ability to coordinate the images from both eyes), which needs stimulation between birth and the age of three years.

A partial listing of research results, while only a sampling of the concept, presents more on this idea of windows of opportunity:

- During the critical period of birth to three years, the foundations are laid for vision, language, muscle control, intellectual development, and emotional development (Wolfe 1996b).
- At twenty-four months, babies who were consistently talked to by their mothers knew 295 more words than those babies of mothers who did not engage their children in conversation (Huttenlochner in Wolfe 1996b).

The growing interest and explosion of information on these windows of opportunity are evidenced by the number of popular magazines that are doing feature stories on the brain and its wiring. Among the current literature, *Time* (Nash 1997b) ran an article delineating wiring windows for vision, feelings, language, and movement and included suggestions for what parents can do to enhance the wiring of windows. *Newsweek* published a Special Edition: Your Child: From Birth to Three, Spring/Summer, 1997, which included a graph of the windows of opportunity for motor, emotions, vision, social, vocabulary, second language, math/logic, and music.

While there is still much to learn about these windows of opportunity, it makes sense to give children rich sensory and language environments, especially in the early years when the plasticity of the brain is most pliable. There is evidence that indicates that if and when these critical periods are absent of any stimulation, the child may develop the skill later but never with ease or proficiency. In fact, when children learn certain skills later, they use different parts of the brain to accomplish the skill, than if they had learned it in the natural course of events (Healy 1990). Further, Kotulak (1996) makes a convincing case for early childhood intervention for the economically, socially, and educationally disadvantaged to guide the massive "rewiring" that occurs in the brain in cognitively beneficial ways. In other words, the sense of threat that invades children's lives in those early years actually causes the brain to rewire itself in ways that engage the instinctive reptilian brain and disengage the cognitive, or neomammalian, brain.

Care and Feeding of the Brain

Lack of sufficient food has grave implications for the brain. The body uses what food there is in the following order: maintenance of vital organs, growth, social activities, and cognitive development (Wolfe 1996b). Interestingly, there are some studies that suggest that if kids have a balance of food types available, they actually select a fairly balanced diet (Shapiro 1997). It is, of course, the adults' responsibility to ensure a proper diet, but there is also information about the workings of the brain that guides the options for nutritious, brain-compatible foods.

If what people eat affects the brain, it's important to know, for example, that neurotransmitters are made of amino acids and that amino acids are the building blocks of proteins. Therefore, protein in the diet before school facilitates brain activity. However, protein by itself tends to also make one sleepy. Protein with carbohydrates (high energy foods) is the better choice for a hearty, brain-compatible breakfast.

Foods sources, beyond the apple a day, include carbohydrates in cereals and grains for energy, chemicals in fruits and vegetables for fighting cancers, fiber in fruits and grains for warding off diseases, calcium in dairy products for teeth and bones, and fat (yes fat) for energy and nerve growth. Since the human brain gets the blood first, it almost always gets the nutrients it needs. The rest of the body will suffer from malnutrition before the human brain will.

Abuses and Addictions

The alert about abuses and addictions is an important one. Without delving into great detail, there are a number of authors that devote their entire focus to the ideas of deprived, defective, damaged, abused, and injured brains. Kotulak (1996) looks at how nature builds the brain and then develops it during early life in response to its environment. He explores how the brain gets damaged from environmental threats, trauma, or alcohol and how aggression is triggered or controlled. The effect of threats on the brain is discussed in length in the following section on emotions.

Wolfe (1996b) graphically depicts the effects of fetal alcohol syndrome on the retardation of brain growth and goes on to explain that this inhibited dendritic growth is not recoverable—the damage is lifelong.

In yet another twist to this exploration of brains that are not properly nurtured, are damaged, or are abused in some way is the emerging evidence about addictions and the role of neurotransmitters in the brain. Researchers are linking the elevation of dopamine (a common substance in the brain that regulates complex emotions and conscious movements) to mood altering drugs (Nash 1997a) that increase/decrease levels of dopamine in the brain. Dopamine is associated with feelings of pleasure and elation and can be elevated by the potent pleasures that come from drugs (Nash 1997a).

New Conclusions

While much of this information about the effects of environment on the brain is emerging, literally, on a daily basis, there is enough evidence to convince researchers that the nature vs nurture dilemma leans much more to the nurture side than previously believed.

Emotions and the Intellect

Just the sheer volume of information available about the emotions (articles galore, audio tapes, whole books, thick chapters within books, and even terminology suggesting an emotional intelligence) provides the first clue to how important the emotions are in the study of the brain. First brought to the forefront by studies done about the limbic system, or the feeling brain, it is well documented that the emotions are the gatekeeper to the intellect (Hart 1983, Issacson 1982, Goleman 1995a, and Kotulak 1996). Sylwester (1995) says, "Recent research developments are unlocking the mysteries of how and where the body/brain determines what it likes, merely tolerates, and avoids. The emotional system emerging from this research is a complex, widely distributed, and error-prone system that defines our basic personality very early in life and is quite resistant to

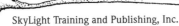

change" (p. 72). With that in mind, teachers should consider the following ideas about threat and challenge and the critical role of a safe, caring, and inviting climate for learning.

Safe Climate

Learners flourish in a safe and caring environment in which learning by trial and error, inquiring minds, and risk taking are the norm. In a classroom that is brain-compatible, the learner feels safe to take risks—to risk making mistakes and being wrong. In the safe climate, the brain is able to function at its highest cognitive level because the learner does not sense threat and therefore continues in his or her cognitive mode. This is the climate most beneficial to enabling learning for all students.

Threat

The emotional brain, according to LeDoux (1996), is the default mechanism to stay alive. It senses threat subconsciously before the conscious mind is aware. In milliseconds, when the brain senses a threatening situation, the heart rate increases, the palms get sweaty, and the body state says something is wrong. What happens is a visceral response and, in fact, the brain probably "upshifts" into a readied state of conscious alert.

This view of the brain sensing threat emotionally before it is cognitively aware and signaling the mind to be on the alert through visceral responses is in opposition to the previously held theory that the brain perceives a threat and "downshifts" to a more primitive emotional state (Hart 1983).

However, in view of the theory of evolution and the concept of the human brain having adapted to its environment for survival, the theory of the emotional brain as a default mechanism makes perfect sense. The human brain's senses have allowed humans to survive as a species.

In brief, emotions drive attention, and attention drives logic and reaction. When people are emotionally on alert, they are attentive; therefore, they are at a higher state of readiness for whatever follows.

Challenge

Emotions have a positive side that can move life from the mundane to the joyful, from the boring to the immersed, from the interesting to the engaging.

In fact, Csikszentmihalyi (1990) describes a mental state of "flow" as an experience of creative oasis, relishing in the complexities and intricacies of a task. This transformational experience is achieved through the challenge of an engaging task or performance. And, while this is the ultimate or peak learning experience, the concept of challenge is an enormously important one in designing classrooms that stimulate brain functions.

Simply put, when the brain faces challenging, intricate, and complex problems, it engages all the parts of the brain. Brain activity is evident throughout the cognitive and emotional realms. In fact, Goleman (1995a) argues that reason without emotional input is impossible. He suggests that "gut feelings" lend great credence to the decisions one makes (Goleman 1995b). Along a similar line of thinking, Wolfe (1996b) discusses the needs for attention, meaning, and relevance for learning to take place. To attend, one must be emotionally secure and comfortably engaged—both are functions of the emotional brain.

In one sense, the emotional component can deter learning to the point of actually rewiring the brain to accommodate continual and unending threat (Kotulak 1996). On the other hand, positive feelings are necessary to give meaning to the experience (Goleman 1995b) and to know deep joy in the learning experience (Csikszentmihlyi 1990).

The Emotional Brain and EQ

New brain research suggests that emotions, not IQ, may be the true measure of human intelligence. As conceived by Mayer and Salovey (in Gibbs 1995), emotional intelligence refers to qualities such as understanding one's own feelings, exhibiting empathy for others, and regulating emotion to enhance living. The following are five elements of the emotional intelligence:

- Self-awareness
- Self-regulation
- Motivation
- Empathy
- Social Skill

Bringing together a decade of behavioral research, Goleman (1995a) hypothesizes that emotional intelligence (a measure of the qualities of the

30

mind) is a better predictor of people's success than the brainpower measured by standardized achievement tests.

A favorite story Goleman (1995b) tells is the study of four year olds. The researcher of the study invited the children, one by one, into a room and told each child that he or she could have one marshmallow right then or could have two marshmallows if he or she waited until he came back. Then the researcher left each child alone in the room. Of course, some children grabbed for the marshmallow the moment the researcher disappeared through the door. Some waited a moment or two, then gave in and ate the marshmallow. Others were determined to wait it out. These children occupied their time with all kinds of diversions. They walked away, covered their eyes so they couldn't see the marshmallow, sang songs, tried to play games, or even fell asleep. When the researcher returned, he gave the children who waited their hard-earned two marshmallows. Then, science waited for them to grow up.

The findings offer astonishingly predictive qualities. Those who had chosen to wait, to delay gratification, were reported to have generally grown up better adjusted and more popular, adventurous, confident, and dependable teenagers than their peers who had impulsively eaten the one marshmallow. Those who had eaten the one marshmallow were more likely to be lonely, easily frustrated, and stubborn as teenagers. They became stressed more easily and shied away from challenging tasks. In addition, when some teenagers from both groups took the Scholastic Aptitude Test (SAT), those who had held out and waited for the two marshmallows scored an average 210 points higher. According to Goleman (1995a) it seems that this ability to delay gratification is a master skill in which reason triumphs over natural impulse, and he sees it as a sign of emotional intelligence that does not show up on an IQ test. However, be aware that EQ is not the "opposite" of IQ, but rather a complementary intelligence. For further elaboration on this idea of emotional intelligence, refer to the section in this chapter about theories of intelligence.

The Brain and the Mind

To distinguish between the brain and the mind is not as simple a task as it appears. Some do not distinguish between the two at all (Sylwester 1995; Jensen 1996a; Rico 1991; Kotulak 1996; Hart 1983), while others are vigorous in their interpretations of each. Bloom and Lazerson (1988) make the unequivocal statement, "The mind is the product of the brain's activity" (p. 6). They see the mind as a function of the brain. Others distinguish between the brain and the mind in similar ways. Barrett (1992) suggests the brain is part of the nervous system and is made of cells and fiber, while the mind is the part of a person that thinks, feels, perceives, and reasons. Sousa (1995) says that the brain is the physical organ in the head protected by the skull, and the mind transcends the head and operates throughout the body. The mind is aware, understands, makes meaning, and is the function of learning.

Brain vs Mind

In its most simplistic sense, the brain is a concrete object that can be touched, but the mind is an abstraction that, perhaps, resides in the brain. The brain is physical, the mind is metaphysical. One can explore the biology of the brain but must explore the psychology of the mind. "Brains, in contrast to minds, are biological—they are given by nature… Minds are cultural—they are the result of experience… Minds, then, in a curious and profound way, are made…" is how Eisner (1997, p. 350) explains it.

In a metaphorical reference to computers that some researchers vehemently disagree with, some say that the brain is the hardware, while the mind is the software. Maybe the dendrites are the Internet of the mind! Speaking of metaphors for the brain, there are references that range from a jungle ecosystem (Edelman in Sylwester 1995; Jensen 1996a), to a symphony orchestra (Sylwester 1995), to a library (Sylwester 1995), to a power plant or a highway system (Tierno 1996). The possible number of metaphors to describe the relationship between the brain and mind is endless; although, each has its own limitations.

Although this discussion of the brain and the mind is somewhat unresolved, for the purposes of this book, the differences are of utmost concern. While information about brain physiology and about how the brain functions from a neurobiological perspective is paramount in educators' work with students, the workings of the intellectual mind seem as important. Educators must be concerned not only with the development of the brain as an organ but also with the development of the intellectual mind. By understanding the intricacies of both, teachers can design learning in brain-compatible, mind challenging ways.

Gender Differences

Gender difference is an important concept to understand. It appears in literature about the brain, and it helps explain how the sexes process information
differently. Gender differences occur in the area of emotions and in spatial
navigation. Certain gender differences in brain functioning have been documented in terms of the location in which the processing occurs (Howard
1994). For example, "male separation of language specialization in the left
hemisphere and emotional specialization in the right helps explain his traditional ineptitude at talking about feelings" (Howard 1994, p. 47). These and
other differences, such as better visual perception and differentiation in
males and greater verbal acuity in females, seem to appear most often after
puberty.

There are differences in the brain chemistry, the length of nerve cells,
the density of nerve strands, and differences in how information is processed
in males and females. In fact, the hormonal levels are the greatest indicators
of gender-related differences in thinking and problem solving. In the male,
testosterone levels correlate with aggression, competition, self-assertion, self-
confidence, and self-reliance. In the female, when progesterone and estrogen
levels are high, math and spatial abilities tend to be lower.

In terms of processing information, Figure 1.17 depicts the most noticeable differences between males and females.

Differences Between Males and Females

Males	Females
• Earlier specialization of right brain; often have more trouble learning to read	• Verbal/linguistic develops earlier; therefore, often read better
• More difficulty talking about emotions	• Can express emotions more easily
• Express themselves in gesture, gifts, and sports	• Express themselves verbally
• Prefer geometric cue (map)	• Rely on memory (landmarks) for finding places
• 15 percent larger brain	
• Lose brain tissue at three times the rate of women	

Figure 1.17

In brief, males and females process sensory input differently, using different parts of the brain. Although the brain is wired in the womb, the differences seem to be more noticeable after puberty.

Gender differences are innately interesting and the more that is known, the more educators are able to tailor learning to the preferences of both genders.

Theories of the Intellect

The preceding discussion on the idea of a brain and a mind leads naturally to an exploration of the theories of the intellect. While the idea of intelligence has been around for some time (Barrett 1992), emergent views of intelligence have abounded in the last few years. The theories of intelligence described here include: Spearman's (in Perkins 1995) theory of general intelligence, Feuerstein's theory of modifiability (1978), Gardner's (1983) theory of multiple intelligences, Sternberg's (1986) theory of successful intelligence, Perkin's theory of learnable intelligence, Costa's (1991) theory of intelligent behaviors; Goleman's (1995a) theory of emotional intelligence, and Coles's (1997) theory of moral intelligence.

General Intelligence Theory: Spearman

This theory is based on the idea that intelligence is inherited and unchanging and is measured by ones ability to score sufficiently on the Stanford-Binet intelligence test. On the Standford-Binet test, an intelligent quotient (IQ score) is obtained by dividing a person's mental age by his or her chronological age, then multiplied by 100. A child with a mental age of ten (based on the test) divided by a real age of eight, times 100 would yield an IQ score of 125. A score of 100 is considered average for any age (Barrett 1992).

Theory of Cognitive Modifiability: Feuerstein

Working with disadvantaged children, Israeli psychologist Reuven Feuerstein (1980) challenges the traditional idea of a fixed intelligence and poses a theory that basically says intelligence is not a fixed entity but rather a function of experience, and it can be changed through guided mediation. This theory undergirds most modern theories of intelligence today, with the concept that human intervention and life experience impact intelligence.

34

Theory of Multiple Intelligences: Gardner

Believing in a factoral model of intelligence, rather than the general intelligence theory, Gardner (1983) posits the theory that there are many ways of knowing, of learning, and of expressing what one knows. Identifying several distinct intelligences, Gardner's theory embraces the verbal, the logical, the bodily, the musical, the spatial, the inter- and intrapersonal intelligences, as well as the intelligence of the naturalist. He sets strict criteria for an intelligence, including biological evidence of brain tissue which processes an intelligence and suggests that an intelligence functions in problem solving and in the creation of products.

Successful Intelligence: Sternberg

Using a factored model of intelligence, Sternberg (1997) in his triarchic theory, argues for three types of intelligence: the analytical intelligence (compare, evaluate, judge, and assess), the creative intelligence (invent, imagine, suppose, and design) and the practical intelligence (practice, implement, show, and use). Based on his emergent theory, the analytical intelligence involves the verbal abilities, the creative intelligence requires quantitative thinking, and the practical intelligence calls upon spatial thinking.

Learnable Intelligence: Perkins

Perhaps the most palpable view of intelligence is presented by Perkins (1995) when he argues for a conception of learnable intelligence. He addresses these questions: Which mechanism underlies intelligence? Can people learn to be more intelligent? What aspects of intelligence need more attention? Perkins basically argues that there is a neural intelligence that contributes to neural efficiency; an experiential intelligence that stores personal experience in diverse situations; and a reflective intelligence that contributes knowledge, understanding, and attitudes about how to use the mind in intelligent behavior. In brief, Perkins makes a case for "knowing your way around" the good use of your mind just as you know your way around a supermarket, an airport, or an opera.

Intelligent Behaviors: Costa

Looking at intelligence in terms of acquired habits of mind, or states of mind, Costa (1991) outlines a set of dispositions as evidence of intelligence. Included in his list of behaviors are persistence, reflectiveness, flexibility, metacognition, problem-posing, accuracy, prior knowledge, precise language, enjoyment of thinking, and transference.

Emotional Intelligence: Goleman

Among the most recent theories of intelligence is Goleman's (1995a) idea of an emotional intelligence. He delineates five elements of the emotional intelligence, including self-awareness (self-confidence and self-decisiveness), self-regulation (controlling impulsivity and handling emotions), motivation (hope, initiative in goal setting, zeal), empathy (reading others feelings, caring), and social skill (influence, leadership, team building). Goleman argues that this emotional intelligence may be more important than IQ.

Moral Intelligence: Coles

Using character development as the basis, Coles (1997) takes the position that a moral intelligence is a valid theory of intelligence. Coles shows how children can become "smarter" in their inner characters and can learn empathy, respect, and how to live by the golden rule through the living example of others and through explicit dialogue about moral issues. The theory is based on how values are born and shaped through the "moral archeology of childhood."

Memory, Learning, and the Brain

It seems necessary to discuss, if only briefly, the relationship between memory and learning. Researchers often refer to memory when talking about learning because the two seem inextricably linked. According to Wolfe (1996b) the learning process involves four interrelated processes: sensory memory, limbic system, short-term memory, and long-term memory.

In this learning process, the senses focus on information (sensory memory), the brain determines if the information is emotionally important (limbic system), the stimulation of the brain cells produces more neurotransmitters as synapses are strengthened (short-term memory), and repeated activation causes changes in the neural networks so messages are sent more effectively and more permanently (long-term memory). In effect, the more these networks of neurons are used the stronger they become and the more easily they are accessed and remembered.

This process is further described by suggesting that memory is linked to three things: attention, meaning, relevance. First, the brain must be aroused and then pay attention to the sensory input to capture it. Wolfe (1996b) states that in terms of attention and focus, the input must hook in within eighteen seconds or the brain loses the experience—the efficient normal brain acts as a sieve to sift out all extraneous information. Then, after the brain has paid attention to the idea, the learner tries to make sense or meaning of the input and attach personal relevance to it. In this way, the learner finds a pattern or another way of "chunking" the input so it can be connected through the neural pathways to other ideas in the brain. That is how the new input becomes part of the long-term memory system.

In another view of the relationship of memory and learning, Jensen (1997b) speaks of four kinds of memory: episodic, procedural, conditional, and emotional. Episodic is memory that is location driven; it is the memory that is linked to a particular occurrence. People's ability to recall in great detail what they were doing when John F. Kennedy was killed or when the Challenger exploded on liftoff are examples of episodic memory.

Procedural memory is the memory that is at work when people find themselves retracing their steps into the room they just left to try and capture the thought that has escaped them. On the other hand, conditional memory is the automatic memory that reminds people, for example, that the stove is hot.

Emotional memory is memory stimulated by feelings. For instance, the memories that rush back to people as they remember a lost love or a childhood sweetheart follow the emotional pathway of neural processing.

Wolfe (1996a), Sylwester (1995), and Jensen (1996) discuss memory in terms of declarative (explicit) and procedural (implicit). Declarative memories are factual, label, and location memories. They define categories and are verbal and conscious. Some examples are names of things, classifications, and groupings.

Procedural memories are automatic skill sequences. They are difficult to make but also difficult to forget! Some examples are riding a bike, typing, grooming, and skating. Figure 1.18 lists the different qualities of declarative and procedural memories.

Declarative and Procedural Memory

Declarative	=	semantic, general knowledge, and labeling (what)
	=	episodic
	=	life experiences, location (when and where)
Procedural	=	habits, motor skills, conceptual skills, automatic skills

Figure 1.18

Several different situations in which memory occurs are listed in Figure 1.19. Take a minute to review the instances that relate to your own experiences.

Learning Through Patterns and Chunking

The human memory is powerful and mysterious. Memory seems to be located everywhere and nowhere in the brain. Yet, all learning depends on memory, including the simple recall of facts and data and the more complex memory system of remembering thinking patterns, conceptual frames, and complex ideas. The idea of "learning and the brain" suggests an intricate relationship between the two.

To assist the learning process, the brain does several other things beyond giving attention and focus to something. The brain creates patterns, or neural pathways, that are linked and connected in larger patterns (sets and subsets) of related information. This is referred to as a pattern-seeking device in the brain and is exemplified in the use of thematic teaching, in which a big idea

HAVE YOU EVER . . .

... gone into one room for something, forgotten what you went into the room for, and returned to the original room where the thought occurred—and remembered what it was you were looking for? (location)

... tried to find a piece of text on a page, knowing exactly where it is placed on that page (upper right corner) but have been unable to find the page? (location)

... read an entire page and then realized you had no idea what you had just read? (semantic)

... driven home and had no memory of the actual drive? (procedural memory)

... recalled a moment in time when a song unexpectedly played on the radio? (emotional, episodic)

... had a sense of "déjà vu"—something has happened before? (episodic)

Figure 1.19

provides an overall pattern for the brain to perceive. The brain is always seeking the big picture—the pattern of thought that is created by repeated use of familiar neural pathways.

Another concept called chunking (clusters or patterns of ideas that fit together) also aids the brain in memory and learning. Chunking (Sylwester 1995) is a phenomenon that is achieved when a coherent group of informational items are rapidly combined and are remembered as a single item. One example of this is the chunk of letters called a word. In a more complex example, the difference between a novice and an expert in a field appears to be that the experts tend to organize information into much larger chunks, while novices work with isolated bits of information (Bloom and Lazerson 1988). An example is the chess master who conceptualizes the whole process, versus the novice who plots the game play by play.

Both these ideas of patterning and chunking are responsible for enhancing memory and, thus, enhancing learning. For that reason, both are recursive themes in the text concerning the brain and the learner in brain-compatible classrooms.

CHAPTER 2

DEFINING BRAIN-COMPATIBLE CLASSROOMS

I think, therefore I am.

—Descartes

CHAPTER 2

DEFINING BRAIN-COMPATIBLE CLASSROOMS

Implications for Schooling

Steeped in the knowledge of the brain and the workings of the brain, Renate and Geoffrey Caine (1991) have synthesized their information into a set of twelve principles about the brain. An overarching four-corner framework and Caine and Caine's twelve principles provide the basis that guide educators' work with children in the brain-compatible classroom.

Principles About the Brain

Caine and Caine's (1991) principles, within the four-corner framework, provide an understanding of how the numerous educational innovations fit with the brain research and sound pedagogy. The twelve principles are 1) the brain is a parallel processor, 2) learning engages the entire physiology, 3) the search for meaning is innate, 4) the search for meaning occurs through patterning, 5) emotions are critical to patterning, 6) the brain processes parts and whole simultaneously, 7) learning involves both focused attention and peripheral perception, 8) learning always involves conscious and unconscious processes, 9) the brain has a spatial memory system and a set of systems for rote learning, 10) understanding and remembering occur best when facts and skills are embedded in natural, spatial memory, 11) learning is enhanced by challenge and inhibited by threat, and 12) each brain is unique.

The Four-Corner Framework

The origin of the four-corner framework is found in an earlier publication, *Patterns for Thinking, Patterns for Transfer* (Fogarty and Bellanca 1989). Based on an editorial by Ron Brandt that appeared in an issue of *Educational*

Leadership in the early 1980s, the idea of teaching *for, of,* and *about* thinking emerged. Robin Fogarty and James Bellanca (1989) thought a fourth element was essential and added the idea of teaching *with* thinking. Thus, the four-corner framework of teaching *for, of, with,* and *about* thinking evolved (see Figure 2.1). These four elements are held to be essential to the thoughtful classroom, to the classroom that requires rigor and vigor in thinking, to the classroom that values cognitive and cooperative structures for increasing student achievement and fostering high self-esteem, and to the classroom that honors the teaching/learning process.

Four-Corner Framework

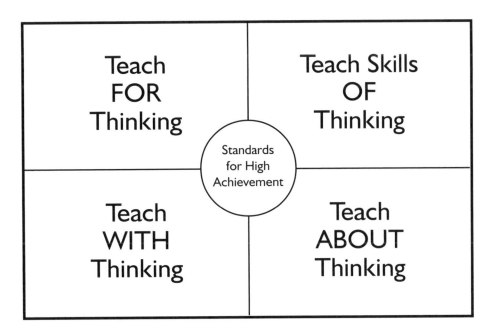

Figure 2.1

The Framework of the Brain-Compatible Classroom

The four-corner framework of the brain-compatible classroom represents the many instructional innovations that comprise current understandings of pedagogy and best practice. In addition, the framework design is developed with a focus on teaching behavior. The teachers in a brain-compatible class-

BRAIN-COMPATIBLE CLASSROOMS
Description

**Setting the Climate
FOR Thinking**

Creating a rich
environment and
an emotionally safe
climate

**Teaching the Skills
OF Thinking**

Teaching life skills
from novice level to
expert level

STANDARDS
FOR HIGH
ACHIEVEMENT

**Structuring the Interaction
WITH Thinking**

Constructing
meaning with
intense, active
involvement of
the learners

**Thinking
ABOUT Thinking**

Fostering application
and transfer with
metacognitive
reflection

Figure 2.2

room set the climate for thinking, teach the skills of thinking, structure the interaction with thinking, and think about thinking (see Figure 2.2).

To further understand the belief that these four elements are critical to the learner-centered classroom and to clarify the implications for the teaching/learning process, a more thorough description of each element follows. In addition, the research base is stated (see Figure 2.3), as well as the names of the leading voices in the literature on brain research and learning theory (see Figure 2.4). The research is then bridged to twelve brain-based principles (see Figure 2.5), enumerated by Caine and Caine (1991), in an attempt to "summarize the accumulated insights... (of the human brain) in a form that is of practical benefit to educators..." (p. 87). The principles also provide guidelines for programs and methodologies which are delineated as implications for learning (see Figure 2.6) and teaching (see Figure 2.7).

Teaching FOR Thinking: Setting the Climate

Teaching for thinking is about setting the climate for thinking (see Figure 2.2). It means creating a learning environment that offers a safe and caring place for all learners, regardless of race, color, creed, age, aptitude, or abilities, to go about the business of learning. In setting a safe climate for thinking, risk-taking is the norm and learners understand that to learn is to make mistakes as well as experience successes. The ideal learning environment presents a rich and stimulating setting for learners to explore, investigate, and inquire.

RESEARCH BASE—PHYSIOLOGY, EMOTIONS, ENVIRONMENT

Research on brain physiology (MacLean 1969, 1978; Orstein & Sobel 1987) and on the actual development of neural networks provides empirical evidence related to setting the climate for thinking. More specifically, two distinct lines of research relate to this critical element. One group of studies (Isaacson 1982; Hart 1983; Mayer and Salovey in Gibbs 1995; Goleman 1995a) concerns the role emotions play in the teaching/learning scenario, and another set of investigations (Diamond 1988) target the concept of enriched environments (see Figures 2.2 and 2.3).

To summarize the critical findings on emotions as succinctly as possible, emotions are the gatekeepers to the intellect. In short, emotional hooks are necessary for long-term learning; negative emotions can become blocks to learning. The findings on the benefits of an enriched environment, although convincing, invariably lead to the age old controversy known as the nature vs nurture argument. Basically, the question is are people born, by nature, with an unchanging brain/mind/intellect or does nurturing through a rich environment impact on the brain and actually increase the neural pathways of intellectual activity? The jury is still out on the actual balance of natural endowments and the nurturing environment, but most researchers agree that the nurturing side of the equation is a critical component.

PRINCIPLES OF BRAIN-COMPATIBLE LEARNING

The following are Caine and Caine's (1991) principles that relate to setting the climate FOR thinking (see Figure 2.5):

Learning is enhanced by challenge: The brain learns optimally when appropriately challenged; thus a safe, rich environment fosters a state of "relaxed alertness" for learning.

Emotions are critical to patterning: Emotions and cognition cannot be separated; thus, positive emotional hooks, such as intriguing questions, enhance learning.

Learning involves both focused attention and peripheral perception: The brain responds to the entire sensory context; thus, in an enriched environment, peripheral information can be purposely "organized" to facilitate learning.

IMPLICATIONS FOR LEARNING

Implications for learning (see Figure 2.6), based on brain research and pedagogical theory, suggest that certain methodologies are more brain-compatible or more "in sync" with how the brain takes in information, remembers it, and, in turn, triggers that information for relevant use. In essence, techniques that set a safe climate and challenge the brain in engaging ways are implied or hinted at by the findings about how the brain works.

Knowing that brain functioning is enhanced by challenge and inhibited by threat and that learning involves both focused and peripheral learning, certain instructional methods and climate setting techniques are dictated for the brain-compatible classroom. For example, higher-order questions, time to think before answering, room arrangement, and enriched environmental stimuli seem more brain-compatible, or conducive to learning, in ways that are easily adapted to how the brain works.

The following are some ways to set the climate in a brain-compatible classroom:

- Be aware of verbal and nonverbal behaviors
- Establish classroom guidelines (DOVE guidelines)
- Recognize emotional and moral intelligence
- Ask high-level questions (fat/skinny; three-story intellect)
- Probe for depth in answers (people searches, wait-time, response strategies, Socratic dialogue)
- Group students diversely (age, ability, etc)
- Schedule blocks of time
- Arrange room for learning
- Create a rich environment (equipment, supplies, sensory input, language stimulation)
- Set up learning centers

IMPLICATIONS FOR TEACHING: SATISFACTORY

Looking at the four-corner framework for the brain-compatible classroom, if the teacher sets a warm, safe, and inviting climate for thinking and authentic student learning, the teacher is doing a satisfactory job (see Figure 2.7). Immersed in a rich, secure environment, students learn. In fact, they learn naturally, in the inductive way they learn outside of the formal school setting.

Teaching OF Thinking: Skills

Teaching the skills of thinking encompasses the life skills that thread through all subject matter content (see Figure 2.2). These skills range from communication and social skills, to the microskills of thinking and reflecting, to the technological skills of the information age, to the skills needed for solving algebraic equations, and for computer programming, and even to the skill training involved in a craft or athletics. Direct instruction of skill development moves through stages: novice, advanced beginner, competent, proficient, expert.

RESEARCH BASE—BRAIN, MIND, INTELLECT

Early research on the brain/mind/intellect focuses on understanding the relationship between the brain and the learning process (Hart 1983; Luria 1976). More current research on the brain and its implications for learning (Sylwester 1995; Epstein 1978; Sousa 1995; Wolfe 1996; Jensen 1996c) are appearing at an incredible rate. In addition, emergent theories of the intellect, including the traditional general intelligence (Spearman in Gould 1981), multiple intelligences (Gardner 1983), successful intelligences (Sternberg 1986), emotional intelligence (Goleman 1995a; Mayer and Salovey in Gibbs 1995), moral intelligence (Coles 1997), intelligent behaviors or habits of mind (Costa 1991), as well as ways of "outsmarting IQ" (Perkins 1995) are inextricably related to this element of the skills that thread through our lives. (See Figures 2.3 and 2.4.)

PRINCIPLES OF BRAIN-COMPATIBLE LEARNING

The following are Caine and Caine's (1991) principles that relate to teaching the skills OF thinking (see Figure 2.5):

The brain processes parts and wholes simultaneously: Bilateralization of the right and left hemisphere processing, though inextricably interactive, allows the brain to reduce information into parts and, at the same time, to perceive and work with it as a whole; thus, immediate application of direct instruction allows the learner to perceive the information from both perspectives.

The brain has a spatial memory system and a set of systems for rote learning: There is a natural, spatial memory that needs no rehearsal and affords instant memory, and there are facts and skills which are dealt with in isolation and require practice and rehearsal; thus, teaching must focus on the personal world of the learner to make the learning relevant, as well as rote memorization techniques to foster long-term learning for transfer. Rote memorization requires more conscious effort to remember because the facts may have little meaning or relevance to the learner. When the brain senses that there is no need to remember (i.e., lack of relevance) it tends to let go of the information.

Thus, rote memorization of isolated facts often needs more explicit work to learn and recall the information, whereas spatial memory has built-in cues that help in the retrieval of the information.

IMPLICATIONS FOR LEARNING

The knowledge that the brain processes parts and wholes simultaneously and that memory is both spatial and rote implies that learning in the classroom needs to be in ways that are compatible to brain functioning. Included in these brain-friendly methods are both direct instruction in skill development, accompanied by application of the learned skills in authentic situations (see Figure 2.6).

The following are ways to teach life skills in the brain-compatible classroom:

- Promote collaboration (conflict resolution, team building, etc)
- Foster critical and creative thinking
- Incorporate technology
- Require performance tasks
- Apply problem solving and decision making
- Support communication
- Build a knowledge base (research, word process, etc)
- Use direct instruction
- Develop skills, concepts, attitudes
- Incorporate embedded application
- Identify peak performance and FLOW

IMPLICATIONS FOR TEACHING: GOOD

Teaching that develops skills, concepts, and attitudes through direct instruction techniques as well as creates a risk-free climate within rich classroom environments is considered to be good teaching (see Figure 2.7). This kind of teaching moves beyond the first element of climate setting and, in fact, combines two essential elements by teaching *for* thinking and by teaching the skills *of* thinking. The reason this combination of elements is considered better or more skillful than merely setting a safe, enriched environment, is because the learning is guided by the teacher explicitly. In this way, the learner is moved more directly to specific realms of learning—to areas of study that the learner may not have approached without intervention.

Teaching WITH Thinking: Structuring Interaction

Teaching with thinking is about structuring the interaction with thought-provoking activities that require intense involvement from the learner (see Figure 2.2). Learning is shaped by an internal process and by social interaction (Vygotsky 1978). Active learning permits the learner to construct meaning in the mind; thus, optimal teaching/learning situations invite the learner to become an integral part of the learning process through hands-on learning as well as dialogue with others. This includes the use of cooperative learning, graphic organizers, and authentic curriculum models such as case studies and problem-based learning.

RESEARCH BASE—ACTIVE LEARNING/CONSTRUCTIVIST

The research basis for the element of structuring the interaction with thinking comes from literature on experiential learning (Dewey 1938; Bruner 1973), the constructivist theory (Piaget 1970; Brooks and Brooks 1993), the active learning theory (Harmin 1994), the work of Caine and Caine (1991) in their synthesis of the brain research and their subsequent call for more connected and interrelated ways of learning, as well as related work about developing a coherent curriculum (Beane 1995). (See Figures 2.3 and 2.4.).

PRINCIPLES OF BRAIN-COMPATIBLE LEARNING

The following are Caine and Caine's (1991) principles that relate to structuring the interaction WITH thinking (see Figure 2.5):

The brain is a parallel processor: Thoughts, emotions, imagination, and predispositions operate simultaneously; thus, optimal learning results from orchestrating the learning experience to address multiple operations in the brain.

Learning engages the entire physiology: Learning is as natural as breathing, yet neuron growth, nourishment, and emotional interactions are integrally related to the perception and interpretation of experiences; thus, stress management, nutrition, exercise, and relaxation become a focus of the teaching/learning process.

Each brain is unique: While most normal brains have a similar set of systems for sensing, feeling, and thinking, the set is integrated differently in each brain; thus, teaching that is multifaceted with inherent choices and options for the learner fosters optimal learning.

Understanding and remembering occur best when facts and skills are embedded in natural, spatial memory: Specific items are given meaning when embedded in ordinary experiences, such as learning grammar and punctuation and applying the learning to writing; thus, experiential learning, which affords opportunities for embedding learning, is necessary for optimal learning.

IMPLICATIONS FOR LEARNING

With an understanding that each brain is unique, that the brain is a parallel processor, that learning engages the entire physiology, and that learning is embedded in the natural/spatial memory, the suggestions for learning are clear (see Figure 2.6). The multiple intelligences approach taps into the uniqueness of each brain, while experiential kinds of learning are useful tools for embedding the learning into natural memory pathways and engaging the learner holistically in sensory stimuli.

The following are ways to structure interaction in a brain-compatible classroom:

- Use cooperative learning
- Utilize graphic organizers
- Target multiple intelligences
- Design integrated curricula
  - Develop thematic units
  - Do problem-based learning
  - Design complex projects
  - Use case studies

IMPLICATIONS FOR TEACHING: EXCELLENT

Teaching that focuses on creating a safe and caring climate within an enriched environment setting; on targeting specific skills, concepts, and attitudes necessary for high achievement; and on intensely involving the learners in active and interactive experiences is considered excellent teaching (see Figure 2.7). When attention is focused on climate, skills, and interaction, students are invited into learning in irresistible ways. Complex tasks, problems to encounter, and time to dig into learning are key.

Teaching ABOUT Thinking: Metacognition

Teaching about thinking is teaching about reflection, self-regulation, and self-assessment (see Figure 2.2). Teaching about one's own thinking is called metacognitive (beyond [meta] the cognitive) reflection. It is about self-awareness and subsequent self-regulatory processing, or self-evaluation. This is the element in the brain-compatible classroom that requires student regulated goal setting, self-monitoring, and reflective actions and reactions to the student and his or her learning. It is the cornerstone of the learner-centered concept that drives personal application and transfer of learning.

RESEARCH BASE—DEEP UNDERSTANDING/TRANSFER

The research basis for this element of metacognitive reflection, or the idea of thinking about how you think and learn, is grounded in literature on cognition (Luria 1976), writings about the mind (Vygotsky 1978), transfer of learning (Hart 1983; Perkins 1986, Perkins and Solomon 1989), mediation theory (Feuerstein 1980), deep understanding (Gardner 1993; Perkins 1986), and metacognition (Flavell in Costa 1991; Brown and Palincsar in Costa 1991; and Costa 1991). (See Figures 2.3 and 2.4.)

PRINCIPLES OF BRAIN-BASED RESEARCH

The following are Caine and Caine's (1991) principles that relate to thinking ABOUT thinking (see Figure 2.5):

The search for meaning is innate: The search for meaning cannot be stopped, only channeled and focused; thus, classrooms need stability and routine as well as novelty and challenge, and the learning can be shepherded explicitly through mediation and reflection.

The search for meaning occurs through patterning: The brain has a natural capacity to integrate vast amounts of seemingly unrelated information; thus, when teaching invokes integrated, thematically reflective approaches, learning is more brain compatible and learning is subsequently enhanced.

Learning always involves conscious and unconscious processes: Enormous amounts of unconscious processing go on beneath the surface of awareness; thus, teaching needs to be organized experientially and reflectively to benefit maximally from the deep processing.

IMPLICATIONS FOR LEARNING

Based on the principles that the search for meaning is innate and occurs through patterning and that both conscious and unconscious processes occur in learning, the call for the mediation of learning is clear (see Figure 2.6). Through reflection, metacognitive monitoring, and explicit transfer strategies, the processing becomes more brain-compatible or aligned to how the brain puts learning into long-term memory.

The following are ways to teach thinking about thinking in the brain-compatible classroom:

- Create personal relevance
- Construct knowledge
- Foster deep understanding
- Make generalizations
- Use mediation strategies
- Embrace metacognition (plan, monitor, evaluate)
- Move to application
- Shepherd the transfer of learning
- Check for understanding (traditional assessment, dynamic assessment)

IMPLICATIONS FOR TEACHING: SUPERIOR

When one enters a classroom in which superior teaching is clearly the norm, it is immediately and visibly evident. In the scenario of superior teaching, the climate is warm and accepting, the environment rich and inviting; appropriate skills are targeted for mastery; and students are actively engaged in experiential learning (see Figure 2.7). But, one other element surfaces beyond the others and the difference in the learning atmosphere is astoundingly obvious. The critical element is self-reflection and self-monitoring. In this classroom, the teachers believe in the innate ability of students to make meaning of their world. That is to say, there are clear and explicit expectations for high standards and high achievement for all students to not only learn, but *to be in charge* of their own learning.

BRAIN-COMPATIBLE CLASSROOMS
Research Base

Setting the Climate FOR Thinking	**Teaching the Skills OF Thinking**
Brain research on physiology, emotions, and environment	Brain/mind intellect and skill development research

STANDARDS FOR HIGH ACHIEVEMENT

Structuring the Interaction WITH Thinking	**Thinking ABOUT Thinking**
Experiential learning, active learning, and constructivist research	Deep understanding, transfer of learning, and authentic assessment research

Figure 2.3

BRAIN-COMPATIBLE CLASSROOMS
Researchers

Setting the Climate FOR Thinking

Sousa (biology)
Wolfe (biology)
MacLean (triune brain)
Diamond (environment)
Hart (emotions)
Isaacson (limbic system)
Ornstein (healthy brain)
Goleman (emotional intelligence)
Mayer & Salovey (emotional intelligence)
O'Keefe & Nadel (memory)
Lozanov (limbic)

Teaching the Skills OF Thinking

Epstein (education)
Hart (learning)
Luria (higher cortical functions)
Sylwester (learning, acquisition)
Sternberg (successful intelligence)
Gardner (multiple intelligences)
Goleman (emotional intelligence)
Coles (moral intelligence)
Perkins (intelligence)
Costa (intelligent behavior)
Mayer & Salovey (emotional intelligence)
Jensen (learning)
Sousa (learning)
Wolfe (learning)
Spearman (intelligence)

STANDARDS FOR HIGH ACHIEVEMENT

Structuring the Interaction WITH Thinking

Ornstein & Sobel (parallel processing)
Healy (active learning)
Gardner (multiple intelligences)
Caine & Caine (connections)
Bruner (learning theory)
Dewey (experience)
Brooks & Brooks (constructivism)
Beane (coherent curriculum)
Harmin (active learning)
Piaget (constructing meaning)
Bloom (active learning)
Goodlad (active learning)

Thinking ABOUT Thinking

Luria (cognition)
Vygotsky (mind)
Feuerstein (mediation)
Perkins (transfer, deep understanding)
Perkins & Solomon (transfer)
Hart (transfer)
Brown & Palincsar (metacognition)
Costa (metacognition)
Flavell (metacognition)
Swartz & Perkins (metacognition)
Gardner (deep understanding)

Figure 2.4

BRAIN-COMPATIBLE CLASSROOMS
Principles*

Setting the Climate FOR Thinking

- Learning is enhanced by challenge

- Emotions are critical to patterning

- Learning involves both focused attention and peripherial perception

Teaching the Skills OF Thinking

- The brain processes parts and wholes simultaneously

- The brain has a spatial memory system and a set of systems for rote learning

STANDARDS FOR HIGH ACHIEVEMENT

Structuring the Interaction WITH Thinking

- The brain is a parallel processor

- Learning engages the entire physiology

- Each brain is unique

- Understanding and remembering occur best when facts and skills are embedded in natural, spatial memory

Thinking ABOUT Thinking

- The search for meaning is innate

- The search for meaning occurs through patterning

- Learning always involves conscious and unconscious processes

Figure 2.5

*Based on Caine and Caine's twelve principles.

BRAIN-COMPATIBLE CLASSROOMS
Implications for Learning

Setting the Climate FOR Thinking

Nonverbal Signals
DOVE Guidelines
Emotional Intelligence
Moral Intelligence
Three-Story Intellect
Fat/skinny Questions
People Search
Wait-Time
Response Strategies
Socratic Dialogue
Student Groupings
Blocks of Time
Year-Round Schools
Room Arrangement

Equipment and Supplies
Sensory Input
Language Stimulation
Learning Centers

Teaching the Skills OF Thinking

Collaborative
Thinking
Technological
Performance
Problem Solving
Decision Making
Communication
Research
Word Processing
Direct Instruction
Developmental Path
Embedded Application
Peak Performance
FLOW

STANDARDS FOR HIGH ACHIEVEMENT

Structuring the Interaction WITH Thinking

Cooperative Structures
Graphic Organizers
Multiple Intelligences
  Verbal
  Logical
  Bodily
  Musical
  Spatial
  Interpersonal
  Intrapersonal
  Naturalist
Integrated Curriculum
  Themes
  Problem-Based Learning
  Projects
  Case Studies

Thinking ABOUT Thinking

Personal Relevance
Construct Knowledge
Deep Understanding
Generalizations
Cognitive Mediation
Metacognitive Reflection
Application
Transfer
Traditional Assessment
Portfolio Assessment
Performance Assessment

Figure 2.6

BRAIN-COMPATIBLE CLASSROOMS
Implications for Teaching

Setting the Climate FOR Thinking	**Teaching the Skills OF Thinking**
Satisfactory	Good

STANDARDS FOR HIGH ACHIEVEMENT

Structuring the Interaction WITH Thinking	**Thinking ABOUT Thinking**
Excellent	Superior

Figure 2.7

SkyLight Training and Publishing, Inc.

Definition of Brain-Compatible Classrooms

Brain-compatible classrooms are brain-friendly places. They are classrooms in which the teaching/learning process is dictated by how the brain functions and how the mind learns. In brain-compatible classrooms or brain-based classrooms, the distinguishing feature is that these classrooms link learning to what is known about the human brain (see chapter 1).

These classrooms are set up with safe, stimuli-rich environments, and a balance between direct instruction for skill development and authentic learning that immerses the learners in challenging experiences. In addition, brain-compatible classrooms tap into the uniqueness of each learner and shepherd relevant transfer for future application of the learning.

To illustrate how brain-compatible classrooms differ from other classrooms, there are several examples that follow:

- Since the brain research *suggests that the brain learns by patterning ideas* or chunking notions that seem to go together naturally, classrooms in which themes are used frequently to connect ideas are seen to be more brain-friendly than classrooms where information is doled out in discrete and separate pieces.
- Since the brain research *suggests an emotional visceral reaction* when the brain senses a threat, testing situations in the brain-compatible classroom are managed explicitly by the teacher to diminish the anxiety and fear and to thus enable the learners to function at their highest cognitive levels.
- Since findings on the functioning of the brain *suggest that learning* involves the entire physiology, real or simulated experiences that tap into the many ways of learning seem to be more brain-friendly. For example, problem-based learning scenarios in which students actually take on the roles of stakeholders seem to be a curriculum model that addresses that brain finding.

In brief, not all classrooms are brain-compatible, or brain-friendly. While they may appear to be places of learning, they may not explicitly target the principles of brain research. The brain-compatible classroom is specifically designed to teach *for, of, with,* and *about* thinking based on the emergent findings about how the brain works and how the mind remembers and learns.

The graphic in Figure 2.8 depicts the essence of the material presented in *Brain-Compatible Classrooms* through a series of themes called brainwaves. Each corner of the four-corner framework comprises two themes, or brainwaves, that provide the focal point for the discussion and strategies, or braindrops, in that area. For example, in the climate corner the brainwaves are emotions and environment; in the skills corner, the brainwaves are types and development of essential life skills; in the interaction corner, active learning and experiential learning are the brainwave themes; and finally, in the metacognition corner, reflection and assessment are the brainwaves that become the overriding themes for that section.

The four-corner framework pictured in Figure 2.9 shows the various dimensions as they are developed in this book. Moving from the bottom of the figure to the top, the six phases begin with the basic overview: setting the climate for thinking, teaching the skills of thinking, structuring the interaction with thinking, and thinking reflectiviely about thinking.

In the second view, the dominant research base for each element is summarized: climate is grounded in the brain research on emotions and enriched environments; research on skills comes from the various theories of intelligence; structuring the interaction is rooted in learning theories, such as active learning and constructivism; and finally, thinking about thinking takes its theory from writings on reflection and application.

The third view delineates the army of researchers referenced in the various arenas.

Climate:	Sousa, Wolfe, MacLean, Diamond, Hart, Isaacson, Ornstein, Goleman, Mayer and Salovey, O'Keefe and Nadel, Lozanov
Skills:	Epstein, Hart, Luria, Sylwester, Sternberg, Gardner, Goleman, Coles, Perkins, Costa, Jensen, Sousa, Wolfe, Spearman
Interaction:	Ornstein and Sobel, Healy, Gardner, Caine and Caine, Bruner, Dewey, Brooks and Brooks, Beane, Harmin, Piaget, Bloom, Goodlad
Metacognition:	Luria, Vygotsky, Feuerstein, Solomon, Perkins, Hart, Swartz, Brown, Palincsar, Costa, Flavell, Gardner

Proceeding to the fourth view, the framework is related to twelve principles that have emerged from the brain research. Based on Caine and Caine's (1991) syntheses, the principles are slotted appropriately to the four-corner framework.

The fifth view focuses on the instructional, curricular, and assessment implications of the elements and their predicating principles. This schema of the educational implications forms the heart and soul of the book, but in brief, the implications for the four elements are synthesized here:

Climate:	Techniques that set a safe climate and an enriched environment
Skills:	Processes that foster thinking, communicating, and getting along with others
Interaction:	Approaches that engage the learner actively and experientially
Metacognition:	Strategies for reflection, application, and transfer

In the sixth and final view, the framework acts as an overlay for teacher evaluation. In this view, teaching performance is depicted as satisfactory, good, excellent, and superior as the various elements are intricately transposed into the high standards classroom.

Together, these six views of the four-corner framework depict the essence of this book and provide a roadmap (see Figure 2.9) to the subsequent chapters.

BRAINWAVES IN THE FOUR-CORNER FRAMEWORK

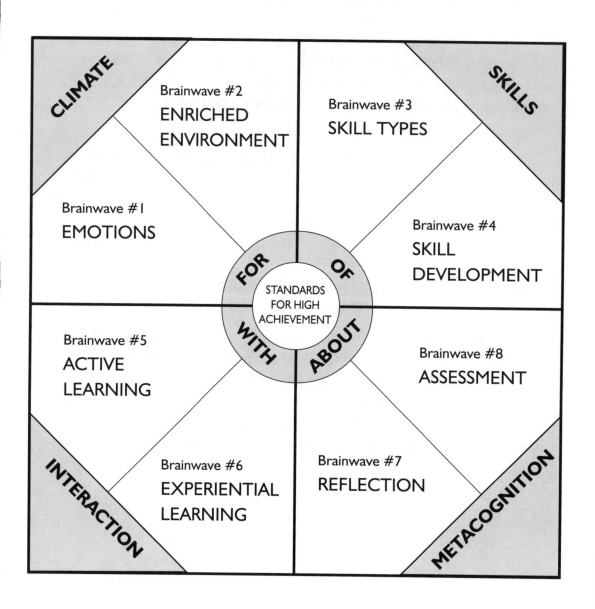

Figure 2.8

THE BRAIN-COMPATIBLE CLASSROOM IN THE FOUR-CORNER FRAMEWORK

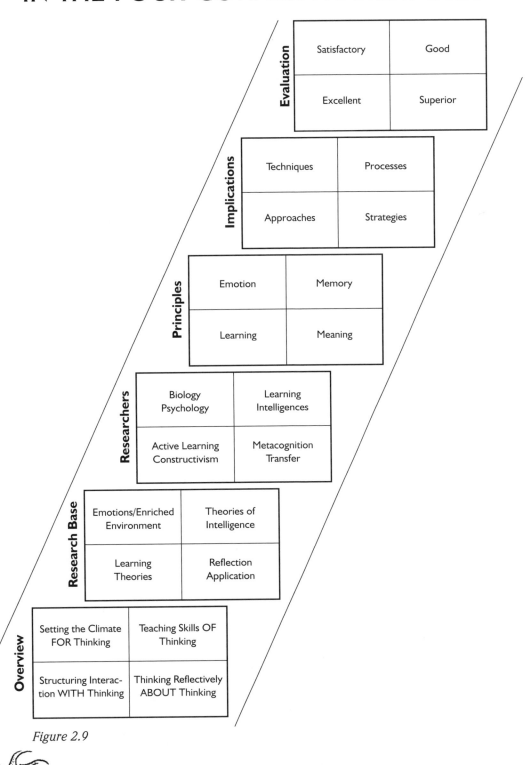

Figure 2.9

CHAPTER 3

SETTING THE CLIMATE *for* THINKING

We must have...a place where children can have a whole group of adults they can trust.

—MARGARET MEAD

KEY

Brainwave: Theme

Big idea that relates to the brain research and/or learning theory

Brainwise: Statements

Quips, statements, or memorable sayings about the brain and learning

Braindrops: Strategies

Strategies, tools, and techniques that help implement instructional methods based on brain research and the learning theory

Brainworks: Activities

Activities or learning experiences for the reader (or workshop participant) to do and to actively think about the presented information

Brainstorms: Application

Personally relevant transfer by reader or workshop participant to tailor for immediate use

Braindrain: Reflection

Reflection and thought about the ideas and processes

SkyLight Training and Publishing, Inc.

CHAPTER 3

SETTING THE CLIMATE
for THINKING

In the discussion that follows about setting the climate for thinking in the learner-centered classroom, the focus is on two interdependent themes: the emotional climate and the learning environment. Within the scope of these two overlapping ideas, this chapter discusses the role of emotions and environment in the brain-compatible classroom and leads the reader into implementation ideas for immediate classroom use.

When setting a warm, safe, and caring emotional climate, two aspects of brain activity are relevant. One phenomenon under the emotional umbrella concerns how the brain viscerally reacts to threatening situations. The other is about engaging the brain with intriguing and inviting intellectual challenges.

To provide an enriched environment for students to learn to flourish, both organizational structures and sensory and language stimuli are involved. Organizational structures range from how students are grouped and how time is scheduled to the room arrangement in the classroom, while the sensory and language stimuli cover the scope from paints, clay, and videotapes to books, magazines, and print-rich materials.

Brainwave
(THEME)

Emotions

To diminish the sense of threat and to establish a warm, caring climate is paramount in the brain-compatible classroom. The existence of a safe learning environment is obvious the moment one enters a classroom that possesses these qualities; it is felt immediately and unmistakably. But what are the qualities that create this sense that it's safe to take risks in this classroom; that it's OK to make a mistake, in fact, it's expected? What is it in this classroom that says this is a place of learning, a place for explorations and investigations? What tells students that this is the classroom for trial and error learning; messy problem solving; constant, continual movement of student directed activity; and lively, animated conversations in which I wonders are the norm? What is it that says that this classroom, unequivocally, belongs to the learners?

Brainwise
(STATEMENTS)

Emotions are the gatekeeper to the intellect.

Challenge causes engagement.

Threat alerts the body.

Braindrops
(STRATEGIES)

A closer look reveals a set of strategies that eliminate threatening conditions that cause a visceral reaction in the body and, instead, invite student curiosity and a sense of challenge (see Figure 3.1). The strategies that concern a nonthreatening climate include nonverbal signals the teacher consciously or subconsciously gives, guidelines that all adhere to, and an understanding and implementation of the principles of emotional and moral intelligence theories. On the other hand, the strategies that set up a challenging classroom climate tend to focus on the verbal exchanges in the classroom, especially the question and response patterns set by the skillful teacher.

STRATEGIES THAT FOSTER EMOTION

Threat Alerts the Body

- Verbal and Nonverbal Signals
- DOVE Guidelines
- Emotional Intelligence
  - Self-awareness
  - Self-regulation
  - Motivation
  - Empathy
  - Social Skills
- Moral Intelligence
  - Empathy
  - Respect
  - Character Shaping
  - Value Shaping
  - Golden Rule

Challenge Engages the Intellect

- Three-Story Intellect
- Fat/Skinny Questions
- People Search
- Wait-Time
- Response Strategies
  - What else?
  - Tell me more
- Socratic Dialogue
  - Activity Justifier
  - Socratic Questions
  - Summary Provider
  - Process Coach
  - Genuine Participant

Figure 3.1

Threat Alerts the Body

All of the strategies listed under Threat Alerts the Body (see Figure 3.1) are strategies that target setting a safe emotional climate in which all students feel free to take risks, make mistakes, and "mess around" with learning. The emotional climate is the key to opening the mind to explorations and investigations. When students feel safe, the cognitive brain is able to engage and process rather than allowing the emotional brain to take over in the face of anxiety, fear, and threat. These strategies are examples of some ways that safe, warm, caring climates might be encouraged.

VERBAL AND NONVERBAL CUES

Subtle verbal and nonverbal cues are key to setting a safe climate. These cues range from facial expression and body language to tone of voice and even to the mobility of the teacher around the classroom. The research on Teacher Expectation and Student Achievement (TESA) provides some invaluable data on the verbal and nonverbal cues in the classroom that affect student interaction (Kerman 1979). Facial expressions and body language can encourage and affirm thinking or discourage and inhibit further thought. Smiles, nods, pats on the back say, "Keep thinking. You're on to something," while frowns, finger pointing, and lack of eye contact mean certain disapproval. Even the absence of an affirming comment is sometimes construed as a negative cue by the unsure student.

In addition, although the words may sound all right, the tone of voice may convey a different message. The comment, "That's an original idea, Joey," might lead to positive feelings if the teacher says it enthusiastically, or it might lead to negative feelings if the student thinks the teacher is being sarcastic and disapproving.

One other obvious signal to students is triggered by the mobility of the teacher. If the teacher remains somewhat stationary, in one spot in the front of the room, the line of the teacher's eye contact, inadvertently, follows that of an inverted T. By continually changing positions in the room, the inverted T also moves, allowing the teacher to focus on different students. This simple strategy encourages more students to be actively involved in teacher-directed discussions and activities.

DOVE GUIDELINES

In some classrooms, guidelines are explicitly developed to create clear and accepted rules of order for all to adhere to. These can be general guidelines for the classroom as a whole or they may target specific exercises or activities. One simple example of explicit guidelines for generating lots of ideas are the DOVE guidelines for brainstorming. The DOVE guidelines call for students to

D — Defer judgment
O — Opt for the outlandish
V — Vast number of ideas
E — Expand by piggy-backing on others ideas

While these guidelines appear fairly simplistic and straight forward, they actually send a subtle message to students that all ideas are valued and that students are to listen to and value other peoples' opinions.

These are powerful messages for students of all ages to learn as they become empowered in the brain-compatible classroom.

EMOTIONAL INTELLIGENCE

Goleman (1995a) has signaled a call to action regarding the emotional intelligence and its impact on learning. His seminal work, *Emotional Intelligence: Why It Can Matter More Than IQ,* outlines five elements that comprise the emotional climate of the learner. These elements include self-awareness, self-regulation, motivation, empathy, and social deftness. Teachers who create a climate free of fears and threats work at building the self-confidence of students, helping them to control their impulsive behavior and to be aware and in control of their emotions. These teachers understand how to develop intrinsic motivation as well as to create a climate for goal setting and feelings of joy in the accomplishment of those goals. These teachers also help kids care about others to the extent that they feel the feelings of the other and foster the skills of team building and leadership.

MORAL INTELLIGENCE

In a similar vein, Coles (1997) builds on the idea of an emotional climate in his current work on the concept of a moral intelligence. In his writings, Coles touches on the idea of learning to empathize with others as a sign of a moral intelligence. In addition, Coles suggests that respect for oneself and others is embodied in the development of a moral intelligence. His concept of a moral archaeology of childhood suggests that morality and the shaping of character and values are the wellspring of the young years—the modeling and teachings children are exposed to in their developmental path toward adulthood. While these are not new ideas, the framing of character traits as a moral intelligence creates a fresh window on morality and its place in the schooling of our children. Is there a moral intelligence and if there is, what is its impact on the climate for learning in the brain-compatible classroom?

Challenge Engages the Intellect

According to the experts (Sylwester 1995; Wolfe 1996; Caine and Caine 1991), when the brain is challenged, it becomes engaged in intense activity. It seems that puzzlement, wonderment, and curiosity cause the brain to "kick in" and begin its intense search for patterns and connections. There seems to be nothing more engaging for the mind than to have a challenging problem to solve. In fact, the brain is a natural problem-solver, continuing to process information even when the person is asleep.

To create models that challenge the brain and engage the intellect, complex thinking is best. The three-story intellect, higher-order questioning, and interactive dialogue such as the people search strategy, wait-time, response strategies, and Socratic dialogue are just some of the critical tools to challenge and engage the brain.

THREE-STORY INTELLECT

One compelling concept that exemplifies a safe/risk challenge for the brain-compatible classroom is captured in the metaphorical structure of the three-story intellect. It is Bloom's taxonomy (knowledge, comprehension, application, analysis, synthesis, and evaluation) synthesized in poetic form by Oliver Wendell Holmes (see Figure 3.2).

THREE-STORY INTELLECT

There are

one-story intellects,

two-story intellects, and three-story

intellects with skylights. All fact collectors, who

have no aim beyond their facts, are one-story men. Two-story men

compare, reason, generalize, using the labors of the fact collectors

as well as their own. Three-story men idealize, imagine,

predict—their best illumination comes from

above, through the skylight.

—Oliver Wendell

Holmes

Figure 3.2

For teachers, the three stories of the intellect serve as easy reminders of the types of thinking required in a challenging learning environment. Of course, students must be able to gather the needed information. But beyond the gathering of facts and data, they must also be ready to analyze, classify, and compare and contrast the information in meaningful ways. It is through this processing that the information becomes meaningful for the student. So, too, in the usual course of events, the final stage of application must play a role. This is the point, after all, of learning—to find uses for the learning that are relevant and helpful.

Thus, in Holmes's version of the three-story intellect, the teacher has a handy reference tool for the students to use in their work. When teachers supply the students with a model of the three-story intellect (see Figures 3.3 and 3.4), the students have a quick guide to reference as they investigate and explore ideas and execute projects.

FAT AND SKINNY QUESTIONS

Another critical element for creating challenge in the classroom is the verbal dialogue of the classroom. The thinking is embedded in the language of the classroom. If the teacher uses questions that call for one right answer or yes/no/maybe-so answers, the depth of the thinking stays at the surface. However, if the questions probe deeper for thoughtful answers, by asking for agreements and disagreements to an idea or by pushing for a clear example of what the student means, then the response becomes more elaborate and the thinking is extended and deepened. In fact, some prefer to label this idea of fat and skinny questions as deep dive and surface questions.

The strategy called fat and skinny questions guides the teacher to ask higher level questions (see Figure 3.5). Fat questions require thought and time to answer. They are not questions that have rote answers in the book; rather, they are questions that have implications that go far beyond the facts and data found in the text references. For example, fat questions ask lots of how and why kinds of questions; they ask students to reason and figure things out, to take a stand and advocate a position, to support that position with facts, to justify and argue that position, and to persuade others to take that position. Fat questions get fat answers.

In fact, skinny questions, often found in text book material, can also be "fattened." For example, when a question requires students to list some

Continued on page 78

Three-Story Intellect Model

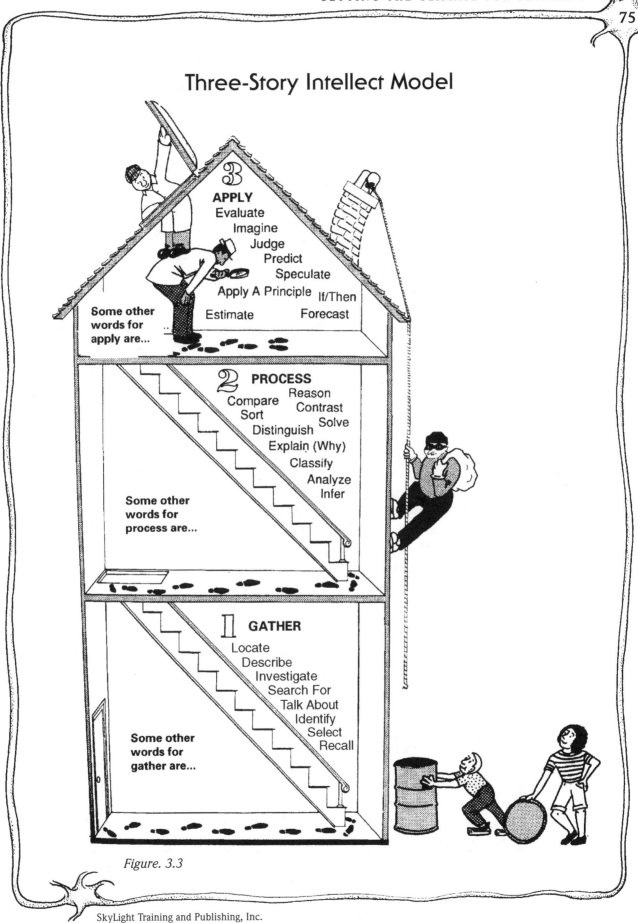

Figure. 3.3

Three-Story Intellect With Multiple Intelligences

3 APPLYING
Try and Test

Verbal: using metaphors, similes, analogies, puns, plays on words
Visual: visualizing, imagining, dreaming, envisioning, symbolizing
Logical: evaluating, judging, refining, creating analogies, reasoning, critiquing
Musical: composing, improvising, critiquing, performing, conducting
Bodily: constructing, dramatizing, peforming, experimenting, sculpting
Interpersonal: debating, compromising, mediating, arbitrating,
Intrapersonal: meditating, intuiting, innovating, inventing, creating
Naturalist: forecasting, predicting, interrelating, synthesizing, categorizing

PROCESSING Crystallize Ideas

Verbal: paraphrasing, essay writing, labeling, reporting, organizing

Visual: sketching, mapping, diagramming, illustrating, cartooning

Logical: graphing, comparing, classifying, ranking, analyzing, coding

Musical: playing, selecting, singing, responding to music

Bodily: rehearsing, studying, experimenting, investigating

Interpersonal: expressing, telling/retelling, arguing, discussing

Intrapersonal: studying, self-assessing, interpreting, processing

Naturalist: categorizing, sorting, relating, classifying

GATHERING 1 Research Project

Verbal: questioning, reading, listing, telling, writing, finding, listening, documenting

Visual: viewing, observing, seeing, describing, showing

Logical: recording, collecting, logging, documenting

Musical: listening, gathering, audiotaping, attending concerts

Bodily: preparing, exploring, investigating, interviewing

Interpersonal: interacting, teaming, interviewing, affirming

Intrapersonal: reflecting, expressing, reacting, journaling

Naturalist: observing, catching, identifying, photographing

Figure. 3.4

FAT AND SKINNY QUESTIONS

Fat Questions

Fat questions require lots of discussion and explanation with interesting examples. Fat questions take time to think through and answer in depth.

Skinny Questions

Skinny questions require simple yes/no/maybe or a one-word answer, or nod or shake of the head. They take up no space or time.

Figure 3.5

SkyLight Training and Publishing, Inc.

Continued from page 74

information (skinny), changing the word "list" to the word "rank" fattens up the question and the level of the thinking becomes more complex. Now, the student must place a value on the list of items. The fat question contains the information of the skinny question and more!

If the words fat and skinny, though embraced and understood easily by students of all ages, are bothersome, teachers can label the two types of questions convergent and divergent, closed and open, or telling and thinking questions. The labels are synonymous—the concept remains constant. Whatever the choice, teachers need to make the students aware of the differences so they become empowered in the use of both types.

In addition, questions can be in-between fat and skinny. Students call these "chubby" questions. "What do you think?" could be a skinny question, and the student could answer, "Nothing." Yet, there is an implied, "Tell me something about your thinking," that suggest a certain chubbiness in the intended response.

PEOPLE SEARCHES

People searches are interactive activities to get people moving about and talking to each other about the topic of the moment. Figure 3.6 uses the FRIENDS acronym to explain why people searches are valued in the high challenge classroom. Figures 3.7, 3.8, and 3.9 are three examples that illustrate people searches on various levels.

To form high-quality questions or statements for a people search, teachers can use the cue words from the three-story intellect (see Figure 3.3). These particular verbs force students into higher mental processes. For example, instead of asking students to list, the statement could require them to rank items. Rank means not only to recall the list but to process that list and place value on each item. Thus, the statement leads to more sophisticated mental processing.

Teachers should try to write the search in such a way that the key issues are spirited "through the back door." The search should not read like a pre- or post-test or quiz. It should be focused, but fun. For example, instead of asking students studying a DNA unit to define genes, the teacher asks them to find someone wearing jeans. The teacher triggers an analysis level of thinking by subtly interjecting a homonym into the search. Students think of jeans and genes which leads them to compare the two concepts. It requires complex thinking, beyond just recall.

FRIENDS: WHY DO A PEOPLE SEARCH?

Focus on content

As students move through the various lessons of the day, it becomes critical that the teacher provide a timely focus for the content to be presented. Carefully designed "search statements" lead students toward the target lesson.

Reinforce learning through articulation

Much of the research in the area of reading suggests that recitation by the student, rephrasing in one's own words, is a powerful way to help place material into long-term memory. By talking with each other, all students have an opportunity to articulate their conceptions.

Invite meaningful interaction

As a teacher promoting thinking for all students in the classroom, getting them to interact with each other about the material is vital. The activity of "searching" out friends to discuss the lesson content does just this.

Exemplify a model of "safe-risk" climate

By structuring the statements on the people search as open-ended and divergent in nature, students are "safe" risking their interpretations of an answer because there are as many answers as there are student "connections."

Note value placed on people as resources

"Cooperation and communication are valued" is the message modeled in this sort of strategy. The teacher is demonstrating the resources available among the members of the group. Student sense that it's not only OK to talk with classmates, but it is expected as part of the learning process.

Diagnose prior knowledge for new learning

As the teacher participates actively in the "search," he or she senses the readiness of the group and notes whether or not the preconditions to the proposed learning are in place. From the information learned in this activity, the teacher adjusts subsequent plans.

Signal priorities of the unit or semester

The teacher can flag the primary concepts, objectives, and goals of the unit (or semester) through the people search. The message to students says, "These are the important things. If you understand these, you have a solid grasp of the material."

Figure 3.6

THE PEOPLE SEARCH AS: A "SPONGE" STRATEGY FOR TRANSITION

Level: Elementary School

Fish Stories

Find someone in our room who...

knows the difference between Flipper and Charlie Tuna.	whose mother loves to cook fish.	can stay under water for 30 seconds.
owns a green scale.	knows someone named Gil.	has touched a fish.
has met a red snapper.	can tell a "fish story."	can make a noise like a fish.

Figure 3.7

SkyLight Training and Publishing, Inc.

THE PEOPLE SEARCH AS: A POST-STRATEGY FOR REVIEW

Level: Middle School

"My Furthest-Back Person—'The African'"

Find someone who...

attended a family reunion last summer.	has a living great-grandparent.	knows what countries his ancestors came from.
can describe what a "family tree" contains.	has a relative who learned English as a second language.	can locate the Gambia River and Annapolis, Maryland on the map.
uses a name different from that on his or her birth or baptismal certificate.	can list the circumstances in which "oral tradition" might be considered dependable.	can defend the African's need to keep his name Kinte and not be called Toby.

Figure 3.8

SkyLight Training and Publishing, Inc.

THE PEOPLE SEARCH AS:
A PRESTRATEGY FOR FOCUS

Level: High School

DNA Search

Find someone who...

has experienced a spiral staircase or slide.	is wearing a zipper.	knows someone named Watson.
knows what to do with a phosphate.	likes to eat sugar.	can make up three words with base in them.
would be a good pair with you.	can name a cell in his or her body that is reproducing right now.	knows an identical twin.
has jeans on.	knows the difference between a female and a male gene.	who ate a protein today.
can name a commercial product that has an enzyme in it.	knows triplets.	knows several symbols in Morse code.
knows a president of a company.	knows someone who uses blueprints.	can take the 1st, 5th, and 20th letters of the alphabet and construct three different words.

Figure 3.9

SkyLight Training and Publishing, Inc.

WAIT-TIME

Asking questions, even in the structured sequence of higher-order questions, does not accomplish the goal of involving all students in the discussion. The strategic use of what the science researcher Rowe (1969) called wait-time must go with the questions.

If there is a single strategy that yields immediate and dramatic increases in student involvement and interaction, that strategy is wait-time. What is wait-time? It is simply SILENCE! SILENCE! MAGICAL SILENCE! That's it—waiting three to ten seconds after asking a question. Teachers can count silently, grit their teeth, and even pick their fingernail! But they need to wait and watch what happens. Not only does the length of student response increase, but the probability of clarification, extension, justification, and on-task conversation increases, too. Students begin to listen to each other. Expecting immediate teacher verification and not getting it, classmates nervously support and defend their own or each other's points of view. They elaborate and give personal, relevant examples. They begin to bridge the new concept to past learning, and they demonstrate evidence of thinking. Student participation noticeably increases with silence. Figure 3.10 itemizes Rowe's (1969) findings.

Wait-Time Study Results

STUDENT BEHAVIOR

1. The length of the students' responses increased.
2. The number of freely offered and appropriate student responses, unsolicited by the teacher, increased.
3. Failure to respond—"I don't know" or no answer—decreased.
4. Inflected responses decreased, thus students appeared to be more confident in their answers.
5. The number of speculative responses increased, thus students appeared to be more willing to think about alternative explanations of the subject matter at hand.
6. Children worked together more at comparing data.
7. Children made more inferences from evidence.
8. The frequency of questions raised by students increased.
9. The frequency of responses by students who were rated relatively "slow" by their teachers increased.

Figure 3.10

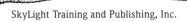

Wait-Time Study Results

TEACHER BEHAVIOR

1. Teachers became more flexible in their responses—i.e., more willing to listen to diverse answers and to examine their plausibility.
2. Teachers' questioning patterns became more manageable; questions decrease in number but show greater variety and quality.
3. There is some evidence that teachers raise their expectations of students who had been rated as relatively "slow."

Figure 3.10a

Although wait-time is not new, it is essential to the thinking classroom. The research documents the effect of "rapid fire" questioning patterns: Students soon learn that the teacher really isn't interested in thoughtful answers, only quick answers. The effective teacher communicates that effective thinking by all is a preeminent expectation. Thus, that teacher waits three to ten seconds after each question before calling on any responder; waits three to ten seconds after the last response before introducing a new question; seeks multiple responses to the same question, even when recall is used; moves close to a student who doesn't usually answer; asks the question to the class, waits, and then calls on the first student; establishes eye contact and cues the students. Figure 3.11 outlines how to use Rowe's (1969) wait-time strategy and Figure 3.12 defines the average teacher.

Based on the seminal work on wait-time by Rowe (1969) the poem in Figure 3.13 summarizes the findings that high expectations for all students is necessary if all students are to achieve to their fullest. As suggested in poem, the average child is just as in need of attention and focus as are the children at the high end or the low end of the infamous bell curve. In Rowe's work, all students were given equal opportunity to respond in depth.

TWO RESPONSE STRATEGIES

There are two simple response strategies that challenge students to keep thinking and to think deeply about an idea. One response that leads to multiple answers is "What else?" When sampling answers from students in a brain-compatible classroom, teachers use the phrase "What else?" to elicit

How To Use Wait-Time

1. Wait at least three seconds after asking a question to let the student begin a response. Say to yourself, "One thousand one, one thousand two, one thousand three. . . ." It sounds simple, but the silence can be deafening the first few times.
2. Wait at least three seconds after any response before continuing the question or asking a new one. This second wait-time recognizes the possibility that the student may wish to elaborate on the initial response.
3. Avoid verbal signals—positive or negative—in asking questions. Among the most common cues are "Isn't it true that . . . ?" and "Think!"
4. Eliminate mimicry (i.e., repeating the response a student has just made).
5. Eliminate verbal rewards (OK, Fine, Good, Right) and negative sanctions (the typical yes, but . . . pattern, in which the teacher completes the answer or restates the question).

Figure 3.11

Average Teacher

- Wait time #1 = 1 second
- Wait time #2 = .9 seconds
- Asks three to five questions in a minute, sometimes ten questions a minute
- Asks 400 questions in short class session
- Repeats (mimics) every student response
- Uses words such as very good and wonderful 25 percent of the time
- Rewards indiscriminately
- Looks for the answer

   Result: The focus is on the teacher, not on the content.

Figure 3.12

multiple answers from a variety of students. By saying "What else?" after one response, students are signaled to "keep on" thinking and are encouraged to generate more novel ideas more often.

THE AVERAGE CHILD

I don't cause teachers trouble
my grades have been okay.
I listen in my classes
and I am in school every day.

My teachers think I am average
my parents think so too.
I wish I didn't know that
cause there is lots I would like to do.

I would like to build a rock
I have a book that tells you how,
Or start a stamp collection
well no use in trying now.

'Cause since I found I am average
I am just smart enough you see
to know there is nothing special
that I should expect of me.

I am part of that majority
that hump part of the bell
who spends his life unnoticed
in an average kind of hell.

—Anonymous

Figure 3.13

Another response that pushes student thinking to more depth is "Tell me more." A truly probing phrase to encourage depth of thinking "Tell me more" is a cue for elaboration, detail, and examples or illustrations of the idea. It is a statement that says the teacher wants to hear about the idea.

SOCRATIC DIALOGUE

While the three-story intellect, fat and skinny questions, people searches, wait-time, and the response strategies are clear conceptual techniques to incorporate into the interactions of the brain-compatible classroom, Socratic dialogue techniques offer still another idea for study and consideration. Socratic dialogue, or Socratic practice, is based on the belief that it is not enough to encourage students to ask questions. Instead, teachers must develop a classroom culture in which the experience of asking questions is consistently rewarded by teacher and peers alike to develop a culture in which the goal is to learn, not just to know. In this ideal classroom, the habit of hiding one's ignorance or lack of understanding is overridden by the need to inquire, know, and understand.

From a practical perspective, according to Michael Strong, in his book, *The Habit of Thought* (1996), there are five roles to the Socratic leader, including activity justifier, Socratic questioner, summary provider or synthesizer, process coach, and genuine participant.

Activity Justifier: The activity justifier provides a clear rationale for why a particular activity is occurring. The rationale can range from enlightenment (Don't you want to be able to think of yourself?) to brain growth (contextual, complex thinking results in greater brain development) to job skills (people with high social and intellectual skills are valued in the workplace).

Socratic Questioner: The Socratic questioner tries to understand exactly why beliefs are held or why one interprets an idea as he or she does (Does that mean...?). This role is like playing the devil's advocate or, in a more positive vein, always being open to another view.

Summary Provider: The summary provider or synthesizer role calls for someone who can pull together the threads of the conversation, provide succinct summaries and insightful syntheses, and clarify the concepts and ideas that have come up (It sounds to me as though...).

Process Coach: A process coach develops an awareness beyond the intellectual content to the processes being used. This person processes during the conversation (speaks to everyone), debriefs afterward (One thing the group could do differently is…), performs individual processing outside the conversation (I was especially impressed with the comment you made about…), and structures related activities (creates self-assessments and extensions to the topic).

Genuine Participant: The genuine participant offers his or her own opinion in appropriate circumstances to build trust in the group and to be a part of the intellectual exploration (My personal thoughts are based on…).

While Socratic dialogue may require more elaboration before many teachers feel comfortable using the techniques, some of these roles are already part of the thoughtful classroom. Lipman, Sharp, and Oscanyan (1980) assembled a comprehensive listing of the types of questions that encourage Socratic dialogue. These questions tend to make student views more explicit, to help them interpret meaning, to become consistent and logical, and to help them see assumptions, fallacies, and faulty reasoning in their thinking. To prime the pump a bit, the questions in Figure 3.14 are the types of questions often asked in the midst of a Socratic dialogue.

Brainworks
(ACTIVITIES)

PEOPLE SEARCH

Create your own people search using Figure 3.15. To practice divergent strategies as you create your own people searcher, scan the examples provided under the Fat and Skinny Questions section. Then, select your topic, select your verbs and write away!

FAT/SKINNY QUESTIONS

Refer to the Brain Teasers People Search (see Figure 3.16) and the people search created in Figure 3.15. Now, review the questions (or statements in this case) and code them as fat questions or statements that require a full, elaborated response or as skinny questions or statements that get a simple yes/no/maybe so response.

Code
F = Fat, elaborate response
S = Skinny, Yes/No response

SOCRATIC QUESTIONING

What reasons do you have for saying that?

Why do you agree or disagree with that point?

How are you defining the term?

What do you mean by that expression?

Is what you're saying now, consistent with what you said before?

Could you clarify that comment?

When you said that, what was implied by your remarks?

What follows from what you just said?

Is it possible that you are contradicting each other?

Could you clarify that remark?

Are you sure that you are not contradicting yourself?

What alternatives are there?

Could you give an example of that?

Are you familiar with incidents of this sort?

Why did you find that interesting?

Are you saying...?

I wonder if what you're saying is...?

So, you see it as...?

Is that the point you're making?

Can I sum up what you've said by...?

Are you suggesting...?

If you're correct, would it follow...?

The implications of what you've said seem far reaching if...then...?

Aren't you assuming...?

Is what you've just said based on...?

What is your reason for saying that...?

Why do you believe..?

What can you say in defense of that view?

How do you know?

Couldn't it also be...?

What if someone...?

Figure 3.14

6 types of questions
- *clarifying*
- *defining*
- *justifying*
- *comparing*
- *evaluating*
- *cause/effect*

THE PEOPLE SEARCH: WRITE YOUR OWN

Level: _____

Topic_____

Find someone who...

Figure 3.15

THE PEOPLE SEARCH: BRAIN TEASERS

Find someone who...

Can tell a personal story about this statement: Emotions are true gatekeepers to the intellect.	Can explain how neurons that fire together wire together.	Can justify the saying, "Your brain is smarter than you are."
Can take a stand on the following: "Practice makes perfect or practice makes permanent?"	Can create an apt analogy for the brain/mind. "The brain is to _____ as the mind is to _____."	Can apply the saying, "Use it or lose it!" to an understanding of how the brain develops.
Can brainstorm five ways to "grow dendrites."	Can agree or disagree with the statement: "Reason rules over emotion."	Can describe their theory on the controversy over nature vs nurture (heredity vs environment).

Figure 3.16

Once the coding is done, revisit your people search and "fatten up" any skinny questions you have.

Using some of the comments from the Brain Teasers People Search (see Figure 3.16), select your position on them using the human graph illustrated in Figure 3.17.

Select a spot along the continuum for each item and think about the intensity of your agreement or disagreement as well as the rationale for your decision of where you are on the graph. For example, using the statement "neurons that wire together fire together," decide how you feel about that idea and take that position in the human graph.

Finally, refer to the human graph idea and take a stand on an issue by choosing a spot along an invisible line that goes from strongly agree to strongly disagree (strongly agree, agree, neutral, disagree, strongly disagree) and justify your position. Think about the need to think deeply about issues and why it is important to take a position. Think about how it feels to make opinions public and how to ease the fear of public ridicule by peers. Think about the feelings and the emotional climate needed for risk taking and how you might facilitate that in your classroom.

Brainstorms
(APPLICATION)

Think of the issues, concerns, and strategies that have unfolded in this chapter about the principles of brain-compatible classrooms—that threat causes a visceral response and challenge engages the mind cognitively and fosters more thought-filled reactions. Then, make a strategic plan to use one of the techniques discussed earlier. Be specific about the application for immediate use in your classroom or work setting. Map the strategy into a relevant use so students have a sense of purpose about why they are using it.

For example, plan a discussion using the Socratic dialogue technique. Introduce the Socratic terminology to students, label the roles as you use them and talk about how Socratic dialogue differs from ordinary classroom discussions.

THE HUMAN GRAPH

Strongly
Agree   Agree   Neutral   Disagree   Strongly
Disagree

Statement: Neurons that fire together wire together.

Figure 3.17

Take some time and reflect on the following ideas. Relate one to a personal experience, and write about the experience as a journal entry.

Braindrain
(REFLECTION)

Idea 1: Emotions rule the mind—they can take over reasoned thinking. Yet, there needs to be some emotional hook to one's thinking.

Idea 2: The sense of challenge is difficult to achieve. There is a fine line between challenge and engagement vs struggle and frustration.

Idea 3: Threatening situations are sensed by the entire body.

■ ■ ■

Enriched Environment

Brainwave
(THEME)

A second and complementary part to setting an emotional climate that is safe is to create an enriched environment that invites learning. In a safe and caring climate, learners naturally begin to explore and investigate. The discussion about an enriched environment encompasses two realms: the organizational, or structural, environment of the classroom and the sensory environment of the classroom. Based on those two arenas, the focus of this section is to delineate the various structures that support the brain-compatible philosophy and the sensory inputs necessary to foster brain growth.

Brainwise
(STATEMENTS)

*It's not nature **vs** nurture but rather nature **and** nurture.*

Enriched environments grow dendrites.

A nurturing environment enhances the gifts of Mother Nature.

SkyLight Training and Publishing, Inc.

Braindrops
(STRATEGIES)

The discussion about creating an enriched environment for learning can be titled How To Grow Dendrites, as it outlines the key environmental factors needed for intellectual development (see Figure 3.18). Couched under the heading Organizational Environment, the discussion leads to descriptions of various student groupings that facilitate learning in natural ways to the actual structuring of the school year and the school day. In addition, things as obvious as room arrangements and the use of the existing facilities are of concern here.

Sensory environment, on the other hand, involves both the stimuli for the senses as well as language stimuli. Included in this discussion are things such as equipment and supplies, learning centers, and other kinds of sensory input.

Strategies for Creating an Enriched Environment

Organizational Enrichments

- Student Grouping
- Blocks of Time
- Year-Round Schools
- Room Arrangement and Facility

Sensory Enrichments

- Equipment and Supplies (availability, accessibility, flexibility)
- Sensory Input (touch, smell, feel, hear, see, and taste)
- Language Stimulation (print rich, language rich)
- Learning Centers

Figure 3.18

Organizational Enrichments

Based on one of the premises set forth here, about organizational enrichments stimulating brain growth, one question begs for an answer: What are the organizational structures that ease the way for learning?

Student groupings, daily schedules, length of the school year, and the learning facility all seem to be obvious concerns for the student-centered classroom, and, of course, the impact of these elements have been studied and documented. Yet, many schools, trapped in the traditions of the past, neglect to evaluate the effectiveness of current practices.

This discussion hopefully will serve as a wake-up call to carefully look at all the components of brain compatible learning, including things as mundane as the room arrangement, as well as the availability, accessibility, and flexibility of equipment and supplies for fostering brain-compatible classrooms.

STUDENT GROUPING

Two ideas jump out in the discussion of how to group students. One is on the concept of multiage groupings which mirrors the natural learning settings of the family and society, and the second is embedded in the writings of Oakes (1993) on the need to detract schools because of the detrimental effects on students. Both of these ideas have been around for a long time, but, based on the recent findings about the brain and learning, new light is shed on old ideas.

The multiage classroom had its beginnings in the one room schoolhouse in which children of various ages worked and learned together. The older ones often mentored the younger ones who learned eagerly from the upperclassmates. The concepts that undergird this idea of natural learning between older and younger students replicates the learning a child has before entering school and after leaving school for the world of work. Why is school the only place that groups kids by their birth age, when in any classroom of eight year olds, the range of learning abilities spans from four or five years to ten or twelve years, at least? The artificial grouping serves no real function, other than management of the number of students. Does this priority need to be reexamined?

In the other related area of tracking students by ability level, the evidence is clear that the detriments of low self-esteem, lack of motivation, and unfair opportunities far outweigh the benefits of more manageable assignments for teachers. Tracking or streaming is an educational disgrace, and the schools where these practices prevail are urged to read the literature and examine the issues related to the tracking practice. If, after doing the research, schools still think that tracking is good for kids, so be it. But the findings for detracking schools are so clear and so convincing that the position promoted here is, unequivocally, to detrack schools.

BLOCKS OF TIME TO LEARN

Although Goodlad (1980) and Sizer (1984) called for blocks of time, clusters of students, and teams of teachers as sensible and learner-centered ways to organize a school, the case for block scheduling and teaching teams, clustered in "houses," or families, has been pioneered by the middle school movement. Recently, however, the concept of moving from a bell schedule to some version of the block schedule is taking the high schools by storm. In fact, it is the most radical change instituted at that level in decades and it is literally shaking the rafters of the high schools.

The shift to a block schedule has been and is being made for solid philosophical reasons. It's not about time, it's about learning. Each school administration and teaching staff seems to have a driving question that leads them into the block concept: What can we do to build relationships in the school? In addition, the actual block schedule adopted varies from school to school based on a balance of needs and constraints: 4x4 (four classes a day that change four times each year), modified 4x4 (four classes a day, with one block using an AB schedule), AB (four classes a day on alternating days for a total of eight classes), modified AB (four classes a day, alternating every other day except on Friday, when all eight classes meet for shorter periods), Copernican (two classes a day of 120 or 240 minutes, changing every forty-five or thirty days).

Block scheduling also often leads to or incorporates the concept of a core teaching team that provides the essential academic disciplines either in traditional subject matter courses or in interdisciplinary courses. The inclusion of the teaching teams as part of the block idea greatly enhances the possibility that teachers do two things more skillfully: enhance the lesson (not merely extend the lesson to ninety minutes) and prioritize and focus on the curriculum (not just cover the content less but spend more concentrated time on the content).

The purpose of the block of time is to enhance learning in dynamic, hands-on ways for deep understanding of key concepts. This requires knowledge, skill, coordination, and commitment on the part of the teachers and is facilitated by collegial support and professional dialogues.

YEAR-ROUND SCHOOLS

One other macroorganizational change that is gaining attention in the educational community is the concept of year-round schooling or year-round education (YRE). While still under much skepticism, the prediction here is that YRE will happen in the next decade. Why? It makes sense in terms of learner-centered schools and the current understandings of how the brain grows and develops. Many students lose academic ground over the summer months, and they may even be losing dendrites. One thing is certain, the neural pathways that are strengthened through concept attainment and concept formation exercises are probably more dormant when lacking the rigor of academic stimulation. While the jury's still out on this innovation, schools fostering brain-compatible classrooms are likely to look into the case for YRE.

ROOM ARRANGEMENT AND FACILITY UTILIZATION

Learner-centered classrooms and the relationship to how the classroom is arranged seem obvious enough. However, grounded in the emergent brain research about the impact of an enriched environment on actual brain growth, the classroom environment issue takes on new dimensions. Is the kindergarten–college classroom learner-friendly? Does the environment invite learners to dig-in, mess around and play with objects and ideas as they explore, investigate, and inquire about their world? Is the room set up in way that invites conversation and collaboration? It's hard to talk to the back of someone's head when seated in rows, all facing the front of the room.

Also, the noise level in a room full of inquiring minds dictates room arrangements that foster small group work and separated areas designated to particular tasks, as well as some accommodation for large group discussions and more direct instruction. Quiet zones can be built in for particular kinds of activities that require a library atmosphere.

This brings the discussion to how the whole facility is utilized. The learner-centered classroom often extends beyond the actual classroom walls, into the halls, the byways between doors, down the hall, and into other rooms, libraries, computer labs, art rooms, and even outside into the courtyard, on the lawns or sidewalks that surround the building. In short, brain-compatible classrooms often are not, literally speaking, just the actual classroom, but the school and even the community may fall within the usable perimeters.

Sensory Enrichments

Moving to the second premise set forth in this section on enriched environments is the idea of sensory inputs. What are the sensory enrichments that facilitate learning? As silly or as simple as it may seem, sensory enrichments range from the equipment and supplies available to the learner, to the opportunities to use the senses, to language stimulation, and even to the incorporation of learning centers that invite learner involvement.

EQUIPMENT AND SUPPLIES

Naturally, the most basic items that enrich the classroom fall under the category of equipment and supplies. Textbooks, paper, pencils, crayons, markers, chalk and chalkboard, staples, glue, paper clips, and tape are essential. In addition, access to a tape recorder; to a record player; to film, slide, and opaque projectors; to video monitors; and to a computer terminal seem necessary in today's classroom.

In the enriched classroom, the supplies and equipment encompass science and technological equipment such as hand-on science kits, lab setups, plants, animals in cages and aquariums, calculators, computers, hard drives, CD ROMs and online services, as well as materials and supplies for the practical and fine arts. These might include paints, easels, kilns, tools, wood, tile, coils, springs, screws, material, sewing machines, drafting paper, T squares, printing presses, and drawing tables.

If the school is unable to supply the kinds of items needed to create a rich and inviting sensory environment, then it falls to the teacher and the students to find a way to get them. In a number of classrooms, the teacher solicits supplies from the parents and students at the beginning of the year or as special projects arise in the course of classroom activities. Notes or letters home bring a surprising flood of goodies to enrich the classroom.

For the classroom to be truly brain-compatible, that is to say, a classroom that fosters brain growth and a flourish of dendrites, the equipment and supplies must not only be in or near the classroom activities, but they must also be available and accessible to students. In addition, students must have some level of freedom and flexibility to use the equipment and supplies in creative ways. While that is not to say that there are no rules or guidelines for use, there is nothing sadder to see, than a room filled with inviting objects that are off limits to the students. Remember, if students are not using it and doing it, the learning is, at best, minimal.

SENSORY INPUT

Based on the five senses that humans use to take in information, the sensory enriched environment is filled with opportunities for students to see, hear, touch, taste, and smell. Much like a children's museum that is organized to be a sensory-rich experience, if the classroom is to be brain compatible, it is steeped with irresistible, intriguing, and curious materials, tools, and objects from various topics. While this sounds more like an elementary classroom, there are great examples of middle, high, and college classrooms that exude with rich stimuli for the curious learner. Figure 3.19 lists several examples of stimuli for each of the senses.

LANGUAGE STIMULATION

Language stimulation involves both a print-rich environment and a wealth of oral language in the form of dialogues, songs, conversations, and articulation among peers, adults, and others. In fact the impact of language stimulation is so critical in the early years that curriculum needs to focus around the idea of what has been called language experience or whole language or the current euphemism of choice, literacy. Regardless of its title, the meaning is clear, language is the doorway to learning.

Language is what sets humans apart from other species in the universe. Language is the result of connected and connecting neural pathways in the brain. While humans think in pictures, thinking is also filled with language that is invisible and inaudible to others. Oral and written language gives voice to our thinking through reading, writing, speaking, and listening.

The classroom that is print-rich is overflowing with books, magazines, newspapers, articles, written papers, poetry, letters, student work, first drafts, final publications, student produced books, big books, stapled booklets, calligraphy, printed pages, handwritten notes, labeled drawings, sketches and cartoons, paperback books, picture books, textbooks, and reference materials, such as maps, globes, dictionaries, thesauri, and books of sayings and quotations. These materials should abound about the room, so students are inundated with printed information. If the classroom shelves are stuffed full and the walls are dripping with papers, students are bombarded with the printed language from every direction.

In addition to the printed word, students in a stimulating language environment are exposed to and immersed in the spoken language in every form.

STIMULATING CLASSROOM ENVIRONMENTS

Sense of Sight: film, video, multimedia, poster, bulletin boards, books, pictures, paintings, drawings, sketches, games, statues, writings, blackboards, whiteboards, cartoons, caricatures, people, places, things, periodic table, beakers, electrical circuitry, bottles, containers, letters, plants and animals, rocks, stones, and seashells . . .

Sense of Hearing: rap songs, rhythm and blues, jazz and classical music, folk songs, Christmas carols, bands, symphony orchestras, bells, choirs, choruses, radios, televisions, head sets, CDs, CD-ROMs, people, peers, teachers, other adults, children, voices, audio tapes, books on tape, foreign languages . . .

Sense of Taste: classroom cooking, snacks, ethnic foods, healthy foods, snack food, junk food, soft drinks, juices, fruits, vegetables, legumes, sweets, starches, dairy products, grains, breads, muffins, cookies, cakes, puddings . . .

Sense of Touch: clay, sand, sandpaper, finger paints, textures, paper, cloth, blocks, puzzles, keyboards, playing musical instruments, paint brushes, canvas, easel, papier-mâché, puppets, dolls, plants, flowers, toys, tools, pencils, pens, markers, crayons, chalk . . .

Sense of Smell: paint, markers, ink, glue, chemicals, foods, paper, chalk, flowers, plants, animals, people, clay, books, aromas, pungent orders, fresh air, rain . . .

Figure 3.19

Included in this concept are oral directions, teacher instructions, discussions, partner sharings, tellings, retellings, poetry readings, stories and short stories read aloud, plays, role plays, monologues, dialogues, questions, responses, dialects, foreign languages, lyrics, raps, operas, and folk songs. The oral language permeates every sector of the classroom as the students learn the lingo for each discipline: Biology—microscope, DNA, genetic code, recessive gene, heredity; English Literature—Victorian, genre, voice, novel, epic, classic, mystery; Geography—plain, terrain, tributary, desert, fjords; Computer Science—bits and bytes, hard drive, CD ROM, disk, floppy, bug, virus; Art—palette, color wheel, blend, brighten, lighten, Cubism, abstract.

LEARNING CENTERS

A fairly common scene in today's elementary and middle school classrooms is the arrangement of learning centers. Learning centers are areas of the classroom designated for certain types of learning experiences. There might be a writing center filled with writing prompts that relate to a classroom topic or unit of study or a math center stocked with calculators, exercises, and problems of all sorts. Sometimes these centers are developed around a current academic theme, or they are organized around Gardner's (1983) theory of multiple intelligences or in more traditional ways such as subject matter content. Chapman (1993) calls these centers FLOW centers in reference to Csikszentmihalyi's (1990) theory of the state of flow that is reached when one is intently engaged in a task.

In the upper level classrooms, these centers may not be stationary but may develop as the unit unfolds. For example, a French class set up a series of four stations for students to rotate through as they apply various techniques to learn their vocabulary words for a particular unit. Also, in a math class, three stations or centers were used to give students three experiences with parabolas. In one center they used the textbook exercise, in another they used circular graph paper, and in the third, they worked with a hands-on project involving wax paper models of the graphed lines. Figure 3.20 extends the learning center examples.

LEARNING CENTER IDEAS*

Imagine how these centers might be filled with sensory and language rich items for the appropriate grade levels and subject areas.

Elementary School:
A Multiple Intelligences Approach to Centers

Word Smart

Picture Smart

Music Smart

Number Smart

Game Smart

People Smart

Self Smart

Nature Smart

Upper Level School: A Biographical Approach

Georgia O'Keeffe Center for Art

Joyce Carol Oates Center for Writing

Maria Callas Center for Music

Madame Curie Center for Science

Wilma Rudolph Center for Health and Fitness

Hillary Clinton Center for Leadership

Emily Dickinson Center for Reflection

Margaret Mead Center for Naturalist Studies

*Taken from Thomas Armstrong's *Seven Kinds of Smart*.

Figure 3.20

Brainworks
(ACTIVITIES)

FOUR CORNERS
Do a four-corner activity using the four corners of a piece of paper. Label the four corners multiage groupings, block scheduling, year-round schools, and teaching teams. Then choose a corner that interests you and write about the idea. Feel free to write about more than one idea. In fact, you can use all four corners, if you wish.

Brainstorms
(APPLICATION)

Sketch on paper your current classroom layout, and label all sensory and language stimuli apparent and visible in the room. Revisit your room design, and apply the ideas about enriched environments by redesigning the room with additional enrichments; use squared graph paper and prepare to discuss enhancements in terms of brain research. Consider including the learning centers in your redesign or as temporary stations that change periodically.

Braindrain
(REFLECTION)

Compare the before and after versions of your room arrangement using the Comparison Alley graphic (see Figure 3.21).

COMPARISON ALLEY
Compare/Contrast

Comparison Alley

Subject:

_____

_____

_____

_____

_____

Differences

Differences

_____

_____

_____

_____

_____

Similarities

Subject:

*Compare two ideas in the corner sections at the top
and bottom; compare similarities in the center diagonal.*

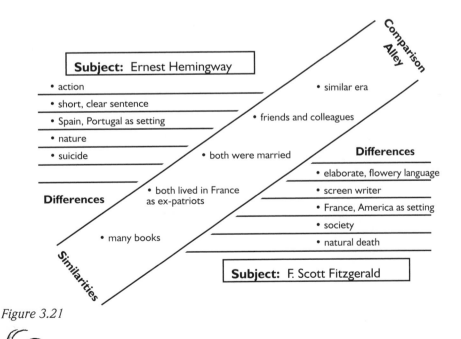

Comparison Alley

Subject: Ernest Hemingway

• action

• short, clear sentence

• Spain, Portugal as setting

• nature

• suicide

• similar era

• friends and colleagues

• both were married

Differences

• elaborate, flowery language

Differences

• both lived in France
as ex-patriots

• screen writer

• France, America as setting

• society

• many books

• natural death

Similarities

Subject: F. Scott Fitzgerald

Figure 3.21

CHAPTER 4

TEACHING THE SKILLS *of* THINKING

A school should not be a preparation for life. A school should be life.

—ELBERT HUBBARD

KEY

Brainwave: Theme
Big idea that relates to the brain research and/or learning theory

Brainwise: Statements
Quips, statements, or memorable sayings about the brain and learning

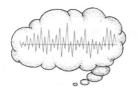

Braindrops: Strategies
Strategies, tools, and techniques that help implement instructional methods based on brain research and the learning theory

Brainworks: Activities
Activities or learning experiences for the reader (or workshop participant) to do and to actively think about the presented information

Brainstorms: Application
Personally relevant transfer by reader or workshop participant to tailor for immediate use

Braindrain: Reflection
Reflection and thought about the ideas and processes

CHAPTER 4

TEACHING THE SKILLS *of* THINKING

A major curriculum focus must be on the skills used to function in and make one's way around this word—the skills of life such as problem-solving and decision making. Skill development is vital to the learning process. Skills are embedded in every discipline, content subject area, or field of study and are the keys to understanding and becoming proficient in any chosen pursuit. For example, in the area of writing, skills of organization, fluency, and structure are necessary to develop a coherent piece of written work. Another example of skill training that leads to proficiency and production is in the field of computer technology. The more adept one becomes at keyboarding, word processing, and graphic designing, the more likely one is to use those skills purposefully in the creation of a useful product.

Teaching the skills of thinking involves two themes: types of skills students need for the rest of their lives and development of the skills in the teaching/learning scenario. The various skills students need can be broken into two major categories: microskills and macroskills. Once the necessary skills are identified, those skills are best taught to students starting at the basic level and moving toward an advanced level or a mastery of the skill.

Brainwave
(THEME)

Types of Skills

In this initial section on teaching the skills of thinking, both microskills and macroskills are discussed. The microskills comprise discrete skills in the areas of collaboration, thinking, technology, and visual and performing arts. Within those realms, the microskills are subcategorized again into such groupings as leadership skills, critical thinking skills, and computer graphics skills. The actual microskills are embedded in these clusters. For example, in a cluster of skills needed for leadership are skills such as visualizing, motivating, and goal setting. Thinking involves microskills such as predicting, classifying, and evaluating.

Macroskills, on the other hand, comprise sets of microskills. Macroskills, or macroprocess, include problem solving, decision making, communication, research, and word processing. To use the macroskills effectively, learners often call upon a series of microskills and abilities. For example, to problem solve, the problem-solver may use the skills of brainstorming, organizing, analyzing, prioritizing, and evaluating.

Both microskills and macroskills are used by the learner in the brain-compatible classroom. Often, microskills are combined into a form of a macroskill. For example, the learner brainstorms, prioritizes, and evaluates with microskills but together they comprise a macroskill of problem solving.

Brainwise
(STATEMENTS)

Use it or lose it!

Déjà vu all over again.

Your brain has been custom-made for you.

Braindrops
(STRATEGIES)

The adage, Use it or lose it! applies to the brain in terms of the types of skills learned and the on-going development of those skills. Although there is a motor memory that enables one to ride a bike many years after the skill was learned and perhaps abandoned, more complex skills improve over time in relation to the frequency and intensity of use. The more the neural pathways are used, the stronger they become and the easier they are accessed.

In the discussion about the types of skills relevant to today's curriculum, one important question dictates the selections: What do kids need to know twenty-five years from now? In response to the question, differentiation is made between the concept of microskills and macroskills, or processes (see Figure 4.1). The microskills addressed in this section fall under the major headings of collaboration, thinking, technology, and performance. From the perspective of the macroskills, or macroprocesses, the following are discussed: problem solving, decision making, communication, research, and word processing.

Essential Life Skills

Microskills

- Collaborative Skills
  - Leadership
  - Communication
  - Conflict Resolution
  - Team Building
- Thinking Skills
  - Creative
  - Critical

- Technological Skills
  - Literacy
  - Graphics
- Performance Skills
  - Athletics
  - Visual Arts
  - Performing Arts
  - Practical Arts

Macroskills

- Problem-Solving Skills
- Decision-Making Skills
- Communication Skills
- Research Skills
- Word Processing Skills

Figure 4.1

Microskills

Microskills are discrete skills, such as predicting, classifying, keyboarding, and even learning to serve in tennis, that require specific attention for proper development. These microskills are the human tools that empower learners in the brain-compatible classroom. With competent and proficient use and in combination with other microskills, the learner is able to function self-sufficiently within the classroom learning environment and throughout life.

To make it easier to examine the various microskills, they have been clustered under the headings: collaborative skills, thinking skills, technological skills, and performance skills. Within those clusters, microskills are delineated for selective use by the skillful teacher.

COLLABORATIVE SKILLS

When thinking about what skills students need in the future, the one area that is often mentioned first is collaborative skills (see Figure 4.2). The number one reason people fail at their jobs is because of lack of social adeptness. They can't get along with their coworkers. Microskills that are included under this collaborative label are the spectrum of social skills of the cooperative learning genre.

Leadership skills such as accepting responsibility, staying on task, and encouraging others, make the list, as well as communication skills such as summarizing and clarifying. In addition, the collaborative skills also include conflict resolution skills such as reaching consensus, disagreeing with the idea—not the person, and team building skills such as sharing materials, developing guidelines for the group, and including others.

THINKING SKILLS

The microskills of thinking fall into two distinct groupings of creative thinking skills and critical thinking skills (see Figure 4.3). The distinction has to do with the type of processing that occurs in the brain. In creative skill processing, the mind opens up to ideas and synthesizes information, while in critical thinking processes, the mind closes in on ideas, takes things apart, and analyzes information. In most situations, both processes are intertwined in the course of brain functioning.

MICROSKILLS FOR COLLABORATION

Leadership Skills

- Check for understanding
- Encourage others
- Accept responsibility
- Stay on task

Communication Skills

- Wait for speaker to finish
- Clarify
- Paraphrase
- Sense tone

Conflict Resolution Skills

- Explore different points of view
- Negotiate/compromise
- Reach consensus
- Respect others' opinions

Team Building Skills

- Include others
- Share materials
- Develop guidelines
- Identify with team

Figure 4.2

SkyLight Training and Publishing, Inc.

MICROSKILLS FOR THINKING

Creative Thinking Skills: Generative, Productive

- Brainstorm
- Visualize
- Personify
- Invent
- Relate
- Infer

- Generalize
- Predict
- Hypothesize
- Make analogies
- Deal with ambiguity and paradox

Critical Thinking Skills: Analytical, Evaluative

- Compare/contrast
- Classify
- Sequence
- Prioritize
- Draw conclusions
- Determine cause and effect
- Analyze for bias
- Analyze for assumptions
- Solve analogies
- Evaluate
- Discern attributes

Figure 4.3

SkyLight Training and Publishing, Inc.

TECHNOLOGICAL SKILLS

The terms "technocrat" and "technoidiot" may seem like flippant and insensitive descriptors, but the impact of either twenty-five years from now could be significant. In the ever expanding, often exploding field of technology, it is imperative that today's students be technologically literate. In the most basic terms, that means literacy skills, such as keyboarding, using spreadsheets and databases, reading technical manuals, and utilizing modems, faxes, e-mail, and online services. In addition, students should be well versed in a graphics program and possibly in animation and multimedia presentation programs. These are the basic skills in today's society (see Figure 4.4). If children exit schools lacking these essential tools, they are ill-equipped to enter the world of work or higher education programs.

PERFORMANCE SKILLS

The performance skills most obvious to talk about fall into the realm of athletic skills or skills needed in the visual, performing, and practical arts. With an understanding of the theory of multiple intelligences and the idea that humans are multidimensional in their profile of intelligences, the skills associated with the bodily, visual, and musical intelligences take on great importance. These skills are integral to fulfillment and joy in living, to multiple career choices, and to recreational options.

Just to touch on the many areas of skill development, athletics encompass the microskills associated with team sports, recreational sports, and health and fitness regimens. The visual and performing arts include the microskills of painting, drawing, sculpting, and filmmaking, while the performing arts include the microskills of dancing, acting, comedic performing, singing, and playing an instrument. Among the practical arts are the home arts, the industrial arts, and designing skills (see Figure 4.5).

Macroskills

Macroskills, or macroprocesses, encompass the various combinations of microskills necessary to complex tasks. These macroskills include activities such as problem solving, decision making, communicating, researching, and word processing. Each of these macroskills is comprised of a series of microskills. For example, problem solving involves the microskills of

Continued on page 118

MICROSKILLS FOR TECHNOLOGY

Literacy Skills

- Keyboard
- Calculate spreadsheets
- Create databases
- Understand manuals
- Use modems
- Fax
- E-mail
- Utilize online services

Graphic Skills

- Design
- Animate
- Create multimedia presentations

Figure 4.4

MICROSKILLS FOR PERFORMANCE

ATHLETIC	VISUAL	PERFORMING	PRACTICAL
Team Sports • Baseball • Football • Basketball • Hockey • Soccer	**Painting** • Watercolors • Oils • Acrylics	**Dance** • Modern • Ballet • Jazz • Ballroom • Line • Square	**Home Arts** • Sewing • Cooking • Home repairs
Recreational Sports • Golf • Tennis • Sailing • Skiing • Skating	**Drawing** • Pencils • Pen/inks • Charcoals • Pastels	**Drama** • Stage • TV • Film • Video	**Industrial Arts** • Electrical • Plumbing • Auto mechanics • Carpentry • Welding
Fitness • Walking • Jogging • Running • Stretching • Yoga • Weight lifting	**Sculpture** • Clay • Papier-mâché • Pottery	**Comedy** • Stand-up • Slap stick • Situation	**Design** • Interior • Industrial • Architectural
	Film • Photography • Movies • Videos	**Music** • Vocal • Instrumental	

Figure 4.5

SkyLight Training and Publishing, Inc.

Continued from page 115

analyzing, brainstorming, evaluating, and prioritizing, while communicating involves such skills as listening, speaking clearly, paraphrasing, and summarizing.

To develop the macroskills, or macroprocesses, the microskills are often taught first and then strung together in appropriate sequences to complete the entire process. The macroskills are, in essence, complex, intricate processes that have layers of microskills built into them. These macroskills, or macroprocesses, are at the far end of the developmental path of skill learning. Macroskills are the result of progression in microskills.

PROBLEM-SOLVING SKILLS

Recently, a high school student was overhead saying, "If there's one thing you learn in this school, it's how to solve a problem. Everywhere you go in this building, they want you to solve a problem." This seems to be an accurate reflection on student expectations. Yet, such a worthy goal is often couched in the aims and objectives of a district. Problem solving, after all, encompasses a realm of situations that range from calculating numerical problems to using problem-based learning or semester-long projects. Problem solving stimulates the mind to make meaning and to search for patterns. It increases blood flow and the dendrites flourish as the brain links new and old neural pathways.

Typical problem solving that occurs in classrooms is encapsulated in activities such as science investigations, math story problems, geometry projects, artistic endeavors, research, essay writing, and foreign language studies. Problems abound in character conflicts in novels, moral dilemmas in history, and in practical ways in labs and workrooms. To organize learning around problem solving is to honor brain-compatible philosophy.

DECISION-MAKING SKILLS

Much like problem solving, the macroskill of decision making is of paramount concern in a rigorous curriculum plan. Decision making permeates every aspect of curricular content. Political and economic decisions are made in the study of social studies, character dilemmas require decision making in writing and literature, procedural decisions are a part of scientific investigations, program decisions are made in computer technology, and decisions thread through dramatic works, sporting events, and game playing. Decision making is also integral when working with others on collaborative projects and deciding on personal goals and objectives.

Again, as with problem solving, it is imperative that students have multiple and varied opportunities to make decisions if they are to become skilled in the process. Decisions as simple as how to prioritize homework assignments to weighty decisions about justifying a decision to vote for a political candidate offer some insight into the realm of possibilities for decision making in the classroom.

COMMUNICATION SKILLS

Without a doubt, one of the most frequently mentioned skills, by both business and industry personnel as well as by people working on building and firming relationships, is the macroprocess called communication. Communication is the ability to share information effectively with others; to be able to clearly paraphrase, summarize, and pass on information from others; and to be an attentive listener, an articulate speaker, a clear writer, and a critical reader. These are not easy tasks to instill in young people, yet their future success in this information society depends heavily on their abilities in these areas.

RESEARCH SKILLS

Another macroskill of primary importance in the information age is the skill of research. To keep up with the overabundance of data and information available to the learner, research becomes a primary tool. It is neither probable nor possible for the brain to retain the massive amounts of information available today. In fact, with information doubling every few years, with the emergence of online referencing and immediate connections to the great libraries, and with primary sources such as museums, institutes, scientists, and researchers, it is all but impossible to access all the information that is out there. Remember, the brain is more like sieve than a sponge. It drops information within nine seconds that is deemed unimportant (see chapter 1).

With the easy accessibility and the continuing explosion in the fiber optics area, the information river is flowing at a rapid and ever-rising pace. Students don't need to know everything, they need to know how to find whatever it is they need at the time. Since the information highway is fast growing into a superhighway, research skills are essential when setting curricular priorities for the brain-compatible classroom.

WORD-PROCESSING SKILLS

Perhaps one of the most urgent skill areas is word processing. To risk an inept analogy, the penmanship skill of yesteryear is the word processing skill of today. Students are lost in the work or study world if they are unable to manage a word-processing program. It is not a privilege in today's classroom to work on the computer, it is a right of every student. Without the ability to compose, to format, to edit and revise, to design, to print, and to produce finished documents, students face grave liabilities in their future career options. With that said, the introduction of this macroskill cannot come early enough in the schooling process. Computers and word-processing software are essential tools for students from kindergarten to college.

Brainworks
(ACTIVITIES)

MICROSKILL LESSON—ANALYSIS FOR BIAS

Analysis for bias is a skill that illustrates the type of thinking skills students need for analyzing written or spoken words, images, and multimedia bombardment.

Use Figure 4.6 to draw possible ideas from three perspectives: viewed from straight ahead, from above, and from below. Think about point of view and how it affects bias. Think of the jury selection process and the particular bias the defense and the prosecutor are looking for in a current, newsworthy court case.

MACROSKILL LESSON—PROBLEM SOLVING

Use your problem-solving abilities and think about the following idea: How would you go about developing a "neighborhood watch" program? Outline the process you would follow to accomplish the project.

Brainstorms
(APPLICATION)

In an effort to apply the ideas about the types of skills students need, survey some students, teachers, parents, and available business people about how they might prioritize the listings of micro- and macroskills. Ask what other skills they might add to the list as they think of them. Advertise the results; comment and discuss how bias might have influenced the survey results.

PERSPECTIVES

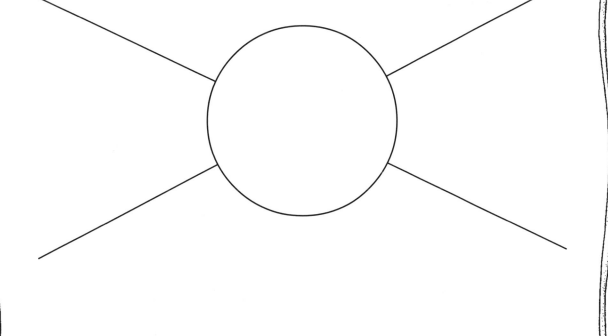

Figure 4.6

Braindrain
(REFLECTION)

Let it all out. Reflect on the types of skills addressed by using the graphic called Drop Down Menu (see Figure 4.7). Learners start at the top of the menu and list all the skills learned, practiced, or used that day. Partners share their lists. If done over time, the priority skills pop out, just like the menu items do with repeated use on the computer.

■ ■ ■

Brainwave
(THEME)

Development of Skills

Practice makes permanent, not perfect. Skill development causes temporary inconvenience, or a dip in the learning curve, for permanent improvement. Teachers must educate for intelligent performance with rehearsal, practice, and coaching. Therefore, practice makes permanent, not practice makes perfect, is appropriate. The practice may be imperfect, but the neural connections continue to strengthen in incorrect or inaccurate patterns. This results in misconceptions and miscalculations. For example, in earth science there are misconceptions about the rotation of the earth, and in golf, several golfers develop a bad golf swing, and it is "grooved" into their muscle memory. In brain-compatible classrooms, the practice is done with constant, consistent, and specific feedback to ensure practice that is permanent is also correct!

Brainwise
(STATEMENTS)

Practice makes permanent.

Do what you can with what you have, where you are.

You can never say no to intelligence.

DROP DOWN MENU
Generating Options

Task or Goal:

Menu of Options

- -

Task or Goal: Read a biography and present vital information to others in the class.

Menu of Presentation Options

Puppet Show Presentation

Quotations on Tape

Comic Strip

Role Play

Video Program

Interview Format

Multimedia Presentation

Figure 4.7

Braindrops
(STRATEGIES)

The development of life skills centers on two levels of skillfulness: basic and advanced (see Figure 4.8). Ingrained in the development of skills at the most basic level is the direct instruction of skills and the developmental path from novice to expert. Imbedded in the advanced level of skill development are the ideas of application, peak performance, and the concept of reaching a state of FLOW.

In the direct instruction model, popularized by Hunter (1982), there are seven phases described in the teaching/learning process which, in fact, may occur in any order and in varying frequency in the direct instruction lesson. These encompass an anticipatory set, a clear objective, instructor input, guided practice, feedback, independent application, and evaluation. In yet another vein, the path of skill development moves from the novice to the advanced beginner, to the competent user, to the proficient user to the expert (Posner and Keele 1973).

Embedded application is the final phase of the developmental process of skill development. It is the use of the skill in an authentic situation. For example, after students have learned the microskills and macroskills associated with word processing, they need to embed the use of the skills in a real project such as a brief science paper or a business letter.

In understanding peak performance, the learner revisits a peak learning experience and a personal peak performance and interrelates the key components of the two.

FLOW, the ultimate level of peak performance, is a state of mental and emotional "flow," like gliding, that is attained when the learner is fully engaged in a personally appealing and appropriately challenging project. FLOW moves from setting goals, to becoming immersed in the activity, to paying attention to what is happening, and ultimately to enjoying the immediate experience. It is the state of supreme fulfillment and brings with it a sense of well-being and satisfaction.

Basic/Apprentice

The Direct Instruction Model, or the traditional Hunter (1982) model of a seven-step lesson design, is basic to comprehensive skill instruction. In turn, knowledge and understanding of the developmental path of skill training is a necessary part to the total package of life skills. Both direct instruction and

PROGRESSION OF LIFE SKILLS

Basic/Apprentice Level

- Direct Instruction Model
  - Anticipatory Set
  - Clear Objective
  - Input
  - Modeling
  - Check for Understanding
  - Guided Practice
  - Independent Practice or Application
  - Evaluation
- Developmental Path of Skill Training
  - Novice
  - Advanced Beginner
  - Competent User
  - Proficient Performer
  - Expert

Advanced/Master Level

- Embedded Application
- Peak Performance
- FLOW
  - Set goals
  - Become immersed in the activity
  - Pay attention to what is happening
  - Enjoy the immediate experience

Figure 4.8

the developmental sequence from novice to expert are seen as brain-friendly or brain-compatible components of the engaged learning scenario.

DIRECT INSTRUCTION MODEL

The direct instruction model for lesson design presented by Hunter (1982) comprises seven distinct parts. These are considered essential to a quality lesson and are often incorporated in lesson design models. The seven steps include: setting the focus, outlining the objective, providing the necessary input, modeling the learning, checking for understanding, guiding practice, and practicing independently. While these do not always follow in order, there is an expectation that these are essential elements.

Anticipatory Set: The anticipatory set initiates the anticipated learning and gets the students to focus and attend to the learning at hand. To get the focus of the students, teachers use images, sounds, surprising comments, questions, quotes, and anything else they can come up with to grab the attention of the students.

For example, a political cartoon on the overhead projector may set the scene for the development of the oral skills of speechmaking. Or the prompt may be a videotaped speech of a politician.

Clear Objective: Students are given clear, targeted objectives that set the purpose for the skill. This often includes an immediate goal and a long-term goal that gives relevance to the learning. Remember, the brain needs a hook to garner attention to an idea. It must have meaning, be relevant, and make sense for the brain to tune in.

Continuing the speech example, the objective statement for the oral skills might say: Learners will demonstrate the essential elements of oral presentation. In turn, the teacher may address the future needs by suggesting the application of the skill in presenting themselves for a job interview.

Input: Often the input phase is textbook information, lecture, video, film, or any form of input that gives the students up-front information for their subsequent work. This phase is at the heart of direct instruction, but without the other phases, this often can turn into too much teacher talk or one-way broadcasts that are not very brain-compatible because they do not foster neural brain activity. It is often too passive a means for the learner to become engaged.

One example of an input phase for giving a speech or oral presentation is to use a videotaped speech and highlight the critical elements. Then, the teacher can create a listing of the elements so the students knows what is expected. The list might include eye contact, voice, visual aid, content, and closure.

Modeling: Modeling is showing or demonstrating the desired behavior or result. The modeling phase sets a standard for the learner and suggests operationally that this is what the learning "looks like" and "sounds like."

An example of modeling is showing completed student artifacts from previous classes or displaying a teacher-made model of the product or performance. With the use of student portfolios, student- or teacher-made artifacts are quite helpful to the learners.

Check for Understanding: Feedback is the breakfast of champions! Everyone wants to know how they are doing, especially when learning a new skill. Remember, there is a learning curve, and when trying something new, things usually get worse before they get better. The feedback from the instructor and from peers is valid. Feedback that is specific and targeted is the most helpful in terms of improving the skill.

In the speech example, the teacher might provide feedback about the volume or pacing of the voice or the impact of the visual. In each case the feedback leads to subtle change by the learner.

Guided Practice: This phase is in the brain-compatible part in which the learner is immersed in the experience with step-by-step instruction. In other words, the skill practice is scaffolded for the learner, taking chunks of learning at a time. In this way, the learner is guided through the various stages with needed information and coaching.

For example, when giving a speech, students may be asked to prepare a one-minute talk for their small group, demonstrating all the elements discussed. As the students rotate through their one-minute talks, the teacher observes and responds accordingly.

Independent Practice or Application: In this phase of the skill development, students practice on their own, incorporating as many of the elements and as much of the feedback as possible. Sometimes this independent practice occurs as homework or as practice outside of the regular class, such as learning a tennis skill or trying a new computing skill. Other times the independent practice may take the form of the actual performance.

For instance, in the speech example, the students may give the speeches in class as independent practice. Or, students may practice with partners, then later give the real speech to the whole class.

Evaluation: At some point, the skill needs to be evaluated for the key elements and ranked or rated accordingly. Remembering that the skill development moves from novice to expert over time, the evaluation is geared to the level of skill demonstrated, knowing that future improvement is likely. The evaluation, therefore, can be formative and ongoing, or it may be summative and final. The evaluation stage may occur during and/or after the skill training.

For example, the students may be rated on a scoring rubric for their speeches. Opportunity to try again or to accept the judgment as is may also be built into the process.

DEVELOPMENTAL PATH OF SKILL TRAINING

Just as the young swimmer progresses from tadpole to sunfish to dolphin, the developmental path of skill training in the brain-compatible classroom follows a predictable path. The path most often suggested is in the terms of novice, advanced beginner, competent user, proficient user, and expert. The developmental path is sometimes confused with the "learning curve." as the learner incorporates the various phases of a skill, the level of skill drops and rises accordingly. Yet the overall path seems to follow a fairly predictable route from awkwardness toward finesse. This path is considered developmental and is observable in skill learning.

Novice: The novice processes the pieces of the skill under study and these parts may not be practiced in any special order. For instance, following the swimming example, the novice may practice the flutter kick, the windmill arm movement, and blowing bubbles under water, when in fact, the sequence was introduced as face in water to blow bubbles, flutter kick, windmill arm movement.

Advanced Beginner: The advanced beginner is characterized by his or her ability to put the skill together in the proper sequence, but the advanced beginner is more interested in the execution than in the results. An advanced beginner asks, "Did I get it right?"

Continuing the swimming example, the learner follows the proper sequence: head in water, jellyfish float, dead-man's float, flutter kick, rotation of arm movement, alternate breathing.

Competent User: The competent user cares about the relationship of the skill to the content. In the case of the swimmer, the competent user now tries to execute the stroke systematically across the pool. The swimmer moves back and forth from side to side, aware of his or her body in the water, how it feels, and how it looks.

Proficient Performer: Once the performer executes the skill with proficiency, he or she is no longer aware of the steps. The proficient performer forgets how to do the various parts, puts the pieces together with grace and ease, and performs the skill automatically. In the case of the swimmer, the proficient performer glides easily down the length of the pool, working the crawl with style and technique.

Expert: Beyond proficiency, the expert forgets everything in terms of the disparate parts. In fact, sometimes the expert cannot properly explain how the skill is executed and will say, "Let me show you." He or she tends to skip steps and to jump to the elegant solution instinctively. The expert swimmer knives through the water with a pace and speed, a strength and quality, and a technique and elegance that is obvious to all.

ADVANCED/MASTER

Moving from basic skill development or apprentice level to advanced or master level is achieved when the skill is easily embedded in a relevant application or when the performance is considered a peak or exceptional performance for the learners, regardless of the skill level. That is to say that an "advanced beginner" skier can have a peak performance for that level of skiing and it would be considered expert for the class at that level.

The ultimate level of advanced learner or master is achieved when the learner attains a state of mental harmony called FLOW. Everything is in "sync" and working at the maximum—everything is flowing.

To teach the skills of thinking in the brain-compatible classroom, the learner is instructed and encouraged to progress toward the advanced/master levels of skill development. Then and only then are the human tools available and accessible when needed.

EMBEDDED APPLICATION

In the development of skills, an initial stage of the advanced level is exemplified in what is called embedded application. This is simply practice or use of the skill within the context of an authentic application. For example, when learning how to recognize and use adverbial phrases, it's one thing to identify the adverbial phrases in a text lesson, it's quite another to incorporate adverbial phrases in one's own writing. To do the latter, one must learn, comprehend, and internalize the skill with depth of understanding.

Of course, even in embedded application there are often improper uses and inaccuracies in the early attempts at the new skill. However, embedded application is what transfer is all about. It gives relevance to learning isolated skills, and it anchors the learning of the skill with personal meaning. When this is the case, the skill becomes more and more automatic as the neural pathways of memory and learning become strengthened.

PEAK PERFORMANCE

The concept of peak performance is often mentioned in the context of the elite athlete or star performer. In the case of Michael Jordan, the great basketball guard for the Chicago Bulls team, the concept of peak performance is what Jordan refers to when he says, "I got my rhythm in the second half" (television interviews following the Bulls game). That means he gave a peak performance at a certain moment in the overall performance. In a similar example, the young phenomenon in the golfing world, Tiger Woods, speaks of having his "A-game going" (television interview following Masters at Augusta, 1997). Others talk of "playing in the zone," "feeling free," "hitting my stride," or even, "flying high." These are expressions that attempt to describe what happens in a peak performance.

All of us have experienced the feeling of a peak performance, whether it be an unbelievable run one morning, a perfect piano rehearsal, or a writing session that wouldn't quit. Peak performances come in other varieties, too. One may experience a perfect sailing day, a magnificent morning painting, or an exquisite preparation of a gourmet dish.

Kids experience peak performances, as well. They talk about how they "couldn't miss" when pitching the baseball game, or they can ride their bike with no hands and move gracefully down the path with obvious ease.

For those who can recall a peak performance, there is no feeling like it. Everything just works! The whole world seems in sync. Bloom (1981) speaks of peak performance in terms of having deep emotional roots. Bloom's statement supports the brain research that suggests that memorable learning experiences are grounded in emotional tie-ins.

FLOW

Csikszentmihalyi (1990) describes an immersion in performance of some kind to the extent that a person reaches a state when everything "flows." When the learner experiences a state of flow, a creative oasis is reached, and the performer takes great pleasure in encountering the complexities of the task. The performer is free of frustration, fatigue, and futility. In fact, the performer has this feeling of intense enjoyment and joy in the performance of the skill.

According to Csikszentmihalyi, FLOW, or achieving the state of flow, involves a series of steps or phrases. To move toward a planned state of flow, or to attain the state of flow, the performer must set goals, become immersed in the activity, pay attention to the process, and enjoy the immediate experience.

Set Goals: Progression toward the attainment of the goal primes the emotional pump for celebration. It is a measurable state and thus, any movement in the direction of the goal provides fodder for further joy in the sense of accomplishment.

Become Immersed in the Activity: To become immersed in a task or project is to see "time fly." Literally, this is the state achieved when time is of no concern. It is so engaging that activities happening nearby go completely unnoticed.

Pay Attention to What Is Happening: The performer who attains a state of FLOW is acutely aware of what is happening during the actual performance. He or she is sensitive to and tuned in to the experience and, at a conscious level, understands that something unusual is happening, similar to the "runner's high."

Enjoy the Immediate Experience: The learner is captured in the moment and relishes the experience as unusual and worthy of conscious and subconscious attention. The performer who attains a state of FLOW remembers it and earnestly tries to recapture it time and time again.

Brainworks
(ACTIVITIES)

BASIC/APPRENTICE
Use the Stair Steps graphic (see Figure 4.9) and track your learning of a sport and the skills involved in the developmental path of learning.

ADVANCED/MASTER
Recall a moment in your life when you may have experienced a peak performance or actually reached a state of FLOW. Share these experiences in a journal. Then, plan a Future FLOW Fantasy. Think about a hobby, an activity, a sport, a career, a career change, retirement, an avocation, or an endeavor that you savor. Then make a plan to follow the steps for attaining a state of FLOW.

Brainstorms
(APPLICATION)

Think about instances in the classroom that lend themselves to developing peak performances for students. Design an action plan of informing students about peak performances and attaining a state of FLOW. Encourage them to be thinking about both and to relate instances when they think they are experiencing peak performances or a state of FLOW.

Braindrain
(REFLECTION)

Reflect on the idea of peak performances with the graphic entitled Chain of Events (see Figure 4.10) and track how the experience evolved.

STAIR STEP

Goal

Climb the stair steps to move toward a goal.
Begin with the first step and proceed to the final stages.

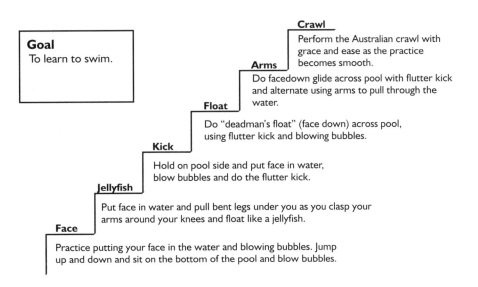

Goal
To learn to swim.

Crawl
Perform the Australian crawl with grace and ease as the practice becomes smooth.

Arms
Do facedown glide across pool with flutter kick and alternate using arms to pull through the water.

Float
Do "deadman's float" (face down) across pool, using flutter kick and blowing bubbles.

Kick
Hold on pool side and put face in water, blow bubbles and do the flutter kick.

Jellyfish
Put face in water and pull bent legs under you as you clasp your arms around your knees and float like a jellyfish.

Face
Practice putting your face in the water and blowing bubbles. Jump up and down and sit on the bottom of the pool and blow bubbles.

Figure 4.9

CHAIN OF EVENTS

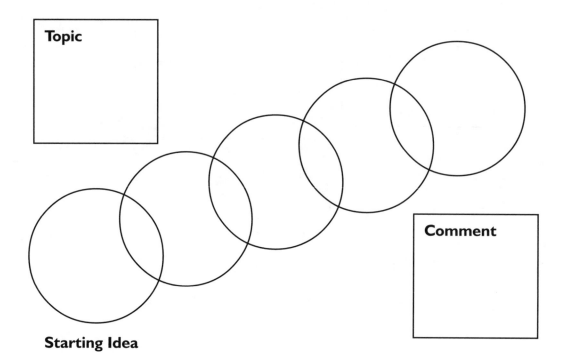

Topic

Starting Idea

Comment

Develop a sequence of events that depicts a picture from beginning to end.

- -

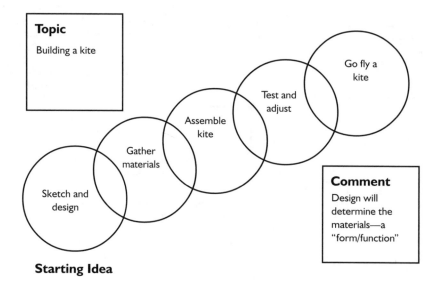

Topic

Building a kite

Sketch and design

Gather materials

Assemble kite

Test and adjust

Go fly a kite

Starting Idea

Comment

Design will determine the materials—a "form/function"

Figure 4.10

CHAPTER 5

STRUCTURING THE INTERACTION *with* THINKING

We are going to have to find ways of organizing ourselves cooperatively, sanely, scientifically, harmonically and in regenerative spontaneity with the rest of humanity around the earth... We are not going to be able to operate our spaceship earth successfully nor for much longer unless we see it as a whole spaceship and our fate as common. It has to be everybody or nobody.

—R. BUCKMINSTER FULLER

KEY

Brainwave: Theme
Big idea that relates to the brain research and/or learning theory

Brainwise: Statements
Quips, statements, or memorable sayings about the brain and learning

Braindrops: Strategies
Strategies, tools, and techniques that help implement instructional methods based on brain research and the learning theory

Brainworks: Activities
Activities or learning experiences for the reader (or workshop participant) to do and to actively think about the presented information

Brainstorms: Application
Personally relevant transfer by reader or workshop participant to tailor for immediate use

Braindrain: Reflection
Reflection and thought about the ideas and processes

SkyLight Training and Publishing, Inc.

CHAPTER 5

STRUCTURING THE INTERACTION *with* THINKING

In keeping with the constructivist theory of learning, which basically states that learning is constructed in the mind of the learner, both active learning and experiential learning are paramount considerations. Active learning requires the intense, hands-on involvement of the learner. In active learning, the learner engages in inquiry, discovery, and exploration; the learner actively interacts with the materials or with others.

Experiential learning is an immersion model that compares to active learning because it involves the learner, but in a more holistic way. Experiential learning is about field trips, museums, outdoor education, simulations, and role plays. It requires authentic experiences that convert to real learnings for learning is a function of experience.

Brainwave
(THEME)

Active Learning

Active learning is an integral part of the constructivist theory. The constructivist theory of learning states that learners construct meaning in their minds; learners process information in their brains and try to make sense of it by finding patterns and chunking bits of information together. The brain is a pattern-seeking mechanism and is constantly and continually searching for connections that make sense. Active learning facilitates that mental processing and the creation and strengthening of the neural pathways, and constructivism holds the long-term learning.

Thus, constructivists, in essence, promote active learning. They believe in intense and interactive methods for students to manage their own learning. In terms of active learning, the models presented here foster interaction with other people (Vygotsky 1978) and interaction with the information (Ausubel 1978). Vygotsky's work suggests that learning occurs first in the social interaction and then internally in the mind of the learner, while Ausubel's work with advanced organizers makes a case for interacting and for representing information visually.

The focus of the active learning section is on using cooperative structures, such as think/pair/share and triads, and on using graphic organizers or visual organizers, such as mind maps and webbing strategies. In sum, the strategies are delineated with discussions and examples. The purpose, of course, is to present a repertoire of ideas to mix and match within the instructional and curricular frames of the brain-compatible classroom.

Brainwise
(STATEMENTS)

Two brains are better than one.

Mind over matter.

Learning is a function of experience.

Braindrops
(STRATEGIES)

If two heads are better than one, why not practice what the adage so insightfully states? When students interact with each other verbally, the dialogue acts as a rehearsal to their thinking. Just as Vygotsky (1978) hypothesizes, the understanding comes first within the context of the social realm, and then it is internalized into long-term memory with deep understanding. An example is when a person verbally tries out an idea on someone else and has difficulty putting his or her ideas into words. Later, the more the person thought about it, the clearer the idea became. And the next time the person tried to talk about it, the words came more easily. It is the active conversation with another and the responses and questions that are returned that push the thinking and foster understanding for both the learner and the listener. Cooperative learning groups are natural structures for this kind of verbal exchange. In cooperative groups, the learner hears what others are thinking and speaks about what he or she is thinking.

In fact, the use of the visual tools create a similar rehearsal for thinking, but in this case, the thinking is visually oriented. The cognitive rehearsal is the reason for and the importance of structuring social interactions and activities for analyzing and synthesizing information with graphic organizers. Figure 5.1 outlines the active learning strategies.

Cooperative Structures

While there are various cooperative learning structures and groupings to use, appropriate to the planned activity, certain decisions permeate every cooperative group. The decisions are about the size of the group (two to four people is ideal), the roles and responsibilities of the members (see Figure 5.2), the expectations for the task, social skills to address (communication, leadership etc), the time allowance, the product or result of the learning, and how the teams are to reflect on their teamwork and the quality of their work.

Active Learning Strategies

Cooperative Structures

- TTYPA...
- Think/Pair Share
- 2-4-8
- Trios
- Cooperative Groups
- Jigsaw
- Expert Jigsaw

Graphic Organizers

- See Saw
- Playoffs
- Bubble Quotes
- Comparison Alley
- Starburst
- The Funnel
- Chain of Events
- Puzzler
- Tri-Pie
- Bridges

- Stair Steps
- Mind Wind
- Brain Drops
- Go to Your Corners
- Drop Down Menu
- Mind Map
- Venn Diagram
- Web
- Flow Chart
- Right Angle

Figure 5.1

These decisions have been organized around the acronym BUILD, Bellanca and Fogarty (1991). The BUILD elements are

B   build in higher-order thinking with complex tasks

U   unite team through common goal

I   insist on individual accountability within the group work

L   look over and reflect and discuss the task and the teamwork

D   develop social skills in the context of the group work

Cooperative Groups: Suggested Member Roles

General Group
Task Leader: Encourages group in task
Observer/Timekeeper: Observes group process
Recorder: Writes and records
Materials Manager: Gets what is needed

Math Group
Calculator: Checks work on calculator
Analyst: Analyzes strategies
Bookkeeper: Checks answers and records time
Inventory Controller: Keeps inventories on materials and
  controls supplies

Writer's Group
Editor in Chief: Tracks progress and sets deadlines
Publisher: Sets guidelines
Scribe: Keeps notes
Author: Supplies the materials

Novel Group
Discussion Leader: Prepares and leads questions
Vocabulary Enricher: Selects enrichment questions
Literary Illuminary: Reads favored passages
Agent: Gets materials

Social Studies Group
Presiding Officer: Presides over the group
Parliamentarian: Observes group behavior
Secretary: Records information
Sergeant at Arms: Keeps the time and gets materials

Science Group
Scientist: Observes progress and keeps times
Researcher: Provides guidelines
Observer: Records information
Lab Technician: Sets up materials and equipment

Primary Group
Captain: Encourages group
Umpire: Observes and reports
Scorekeeper: Writes down information
Runner: Gets what is needed

Figure 5.2

SkyLight Training and Publishing, Inc.

While resources abound in the area of cooperative learning, ranging from the work of the Johnson brothers (1986) and their conceptual work, to Kagan (1977) and his structures, to Slavin (1983) and his work with team tasks and content, to Sharan and Sharan's (1976) work on group investigations, the complementary resource reference here is *Blueprints for Thinking in a Cooperative Classroom,* by Bellanca and Fogarty (1991).

In the meantime, a selection of various group structures are presented for immediate use in the brain-compatible classroom.

TTYPA...(WEAVER AND COTRELL 1986)

Turn to Your Partner and... is a simple, informal interactive strategy that teachers can use as a "pause and think" time during a longer discussion, lecture, film, etc. It signals the brain to tune in and think by creating a need for dialogue. Then, the outer thinking becomes inner thinking.

THINK/PAIR/SHARE (LYMAN AND MCTIGHE 1988)

Students who work with partners 1) think on their own, 2) put their heads together, and 3) share their ideas with each other and other pairs. Sometimes the pair is even required to agree on one idea to share. This is a viable strategy for getting students to think first and then to talk and share their ideas in a small, safe setting of one other person.

2-4-8 (BELLANCA AND FOGARTY 1988)

The 2-4-8 interaction invites two people, A and B, to talk and listen; then A and B join two others, C and D, to create a foursome. In the foursome, A tells about B, B about A, and so on. The four people have to listen in the first interaction in order to share in the second grouping. Now, the foursome joins another foursome, for a group of eight. Again, in this larger group, no one tells his or her own story, but shares one they have not told before. The 2-4-8 sets the scene for listening to each other and for paraphrasing and synthesizing information because as the group grows, the stories get shorter.

COOPERATIVE GROUPS (JOHNSON AND JOHNSON 1986)

The students are formally assigned to a small groups of three or four. Care is taken to make the group as heterogeneous as possible—the more diverse the group the richer the thinking. In addition, roles (recorder, reporter, etc) and responsibilities are sorted out, either by teacher assignment or through some structured scheme such as drawing a card or number. The task, time, tools, etc are clarified, the social skill is targeted, and the groups get to work. After completing the task, the groups share their products with each other by sampling ideas or by sharing with one other group. Then they take a moment to reflect about their group work.

JIGSAW (ARONSON 1978)

The jigsaw strategy (see Figure 5.3) is a division of labor in which several students work in a group and each takes one part of the puzzle or task to complete. When the students finish and they each contribute their part of the jigsaw, and all the pieces of the puzzle come together. In this way, the members of the group must trust each other and be interdependent in achieving their goal.

The key to the jigsaw is when students bring the pieces together. The saying goes, Each one must teach one. Many people know that it is through teaching that the one teaching truly understands what it is he or she is teaching. If someone is responsible to teach another, the one doing the teaching really digs in and ferrets out a clear understanding, because it's hard to teach something you don't understand.

Thus, the power in the jigsaw is in helping students decide what they need to share in the jigsaw and how they can share it so every group member understands it. The jigsaw is a somewhat sophisticated strategy and may need lots of scaffolding by the teacher.

EXPERT JIGSAW (ARONSON 1978)

Just like the jigsaw, the work is divided up among the base-group members. However, in the expert jigsaw (see Figure 5.4), members from each base group having the same part, come together as experts on that one part. Together the "expert group" works to decide what is important to take back to the base groups and how the members will share that information.

For example, if the base groups jigsaw three parts (ones, twos, and threes), the ones from all the base groups meet, the twos from all the base groups meet, and the threes from all the base groups meet. After doing preliminary work in the expert groups, the members return to their base groups to do the teaching rounds. In this way, the base-group members have the advantage of collaborating on each of their jigsawed parts.

JIGSAW

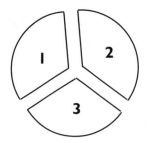

Base Group
(Members divide work.)

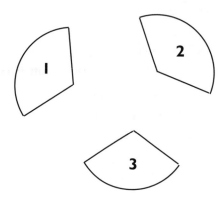

Individual Work
(Members decide what's important and how to teach their fellow group members.)

Base Group
(Members teach each other.)

Figure 5.3

EXPERT JIGSAW

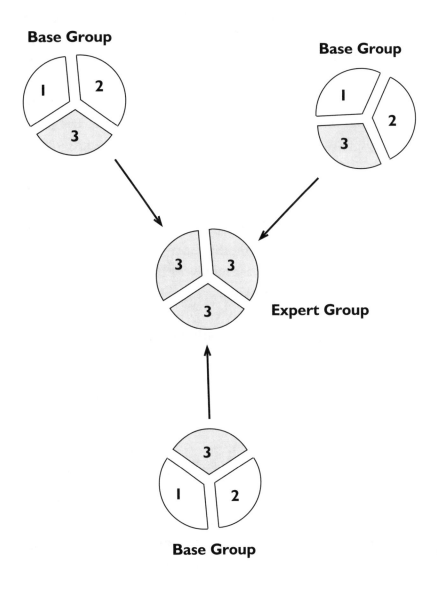

Figure 5.4

Graphic Organizers

The use of graphic organizers is a strategy often seen in today's classrooms as the interaction with the information that makes the thinking visible to the students. The graphics most common among the available spectrum are the concept map (or mind map), the web, the Venn diagram, and the sequence or flow chart, and the right-angle thinking model. Students are familiar with these and are often expected to use them in their cooperative group work. When they use them in the small groups, they may draw the graphics on large newsprint and create a model for the group to work with. Because the drawing is large enough for everyone in the small group to see, the activity invites participation by the members. This gives them a tool to use as they do their thinking.

While teachers often are the ones to assign a particular graphic, eventually, after the students have been introduced to a repertoire of graphic organizers, the groups should decide on the most appropriate one to use to represent the information at hand. This empowers the students to think about how they want to represent their thinking.

There are twenty graphic organizers presented in Figures 5.5 through 5.24 for teachers and students to play around with and, hopefully, to spark further ideas for students to generate original graphics to suit their needs. The following pages show a completed example, as well as a blank graphic for duplication or reproduction (except for the Mind Map, which is a free flowing thought process) on large paper.

Brainworks
(ACTIVITIES)

DEALING WITH PARADOX
Lead the students through the levels of activities moving from the concrete to the representational to the abstract. Use small groups and graphic organizers to develop the active learning experience.

Concrete Experience
Organize students into small groups. Have one student in each group put on a vest and a sports jacket or blazer over the vest. Challenge the groups to problem solve a way for the subjects to remove the vest without removing the

continued on page 167

GRAPHIC ORGANIZERS

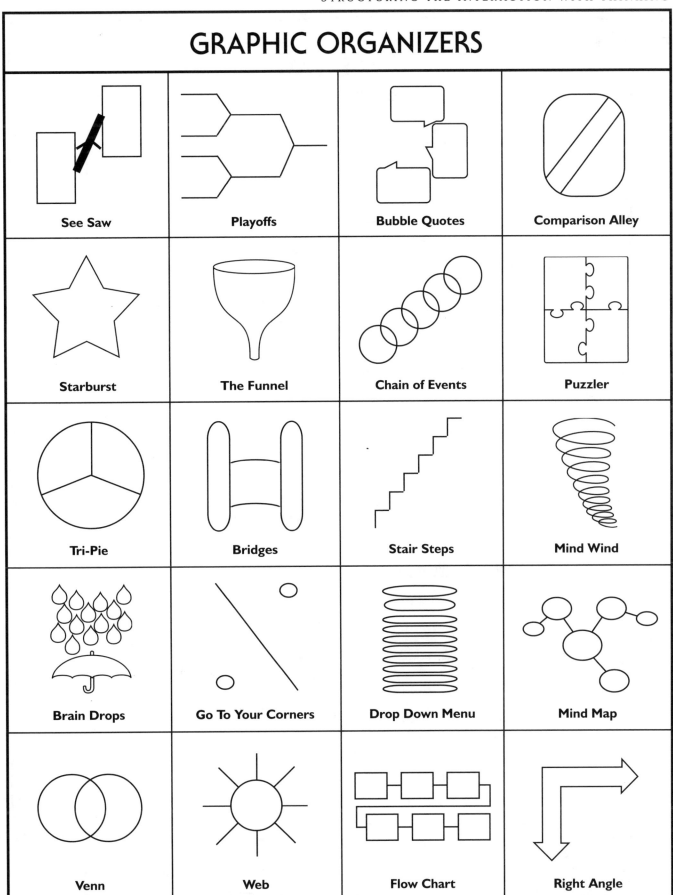

See Saw	**Playoffs**	**Bubble Quotes**	**Comparison Alley**
Starburst	**The Funnel**	**Chain of Events**	**Puzzler**
Tri-Pie	**Bridges**	**Stair Steps**	**Mind Wind**
Brain Drops	**Go To Your Corners**	**Drop Down Menu**	**Mind Map**
Venn	**Web**	**Flow Chart**	**Right Angle**

Figure 5.5   SkyLight Training and Publishing, Inc.

SEE SAW
Yeah but . . . what if?

Problem/Challenge . . .

What if? . . .

Yeah, but . . .

*See saw some ideas by looking at the objections (yeah, but)
and ways to overcome the objections (what if).*

Problem/Challenge . . .

To join the Internet;
go online . . . or to wait

What if? . . .

- you try it for 3 months
- monitor yourself by
  setting time limits
- research self-censoring or
  parental censoring
  devices
- join now and "pioneer"
  and "explore"

Yeah, but . . .

- it costs $20/month
- there is limited access
- the Internet provides
  unedited and uncensored
  information
- I'm afraid I'll get hooked
  on it
- it's not perfected yet

Figure 5.6

PLAYOFFS
Either/Or

Topic or Idea

Select and refine ideas by choosing either/or items until an idea is crystallized.
Justify your choices.

- -

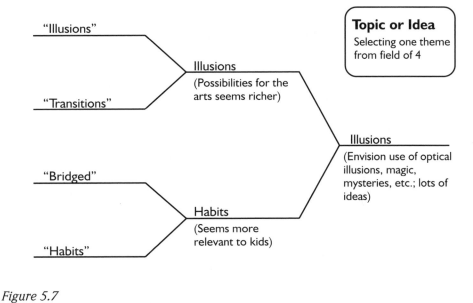

"Illusions"

"Transitions"

Illusions
(Possibilities for the arts seems richer)

Topic or Idea
Selecting one theme from field of 4

Illusions
(Envision use of optical illusions, magic, mysteries, etc.; lots of ideas)

"Bridged"

"Habits"

Habits
(Seems more relevant to kids)

Figure 5.7

BUBBLE QUOTES
Logical Response

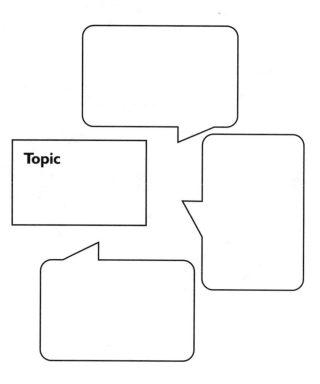

Topic

Create three perspectives and tell the role the person plays.

- -

I have rights, too. I'm not a child.
(Teen)

Topic
Community curfews

I'll feel better knowing my teen is home safe and sound.
(Parent)

There will be fewer crimes and less graffiti.
(Police Officer)

Figure 5.8

COMPARISON ALLEY
Compare/Contrast

Comparison Alley

Subject:

_____

_____

_____

_____

_____

_____

Differences

Differences

_____

_____

_____

_____

_____

Similarities

Subject:

*Compare two ideas in the corner sections at the top
and bottom; compare similarities in the center diagonal.*

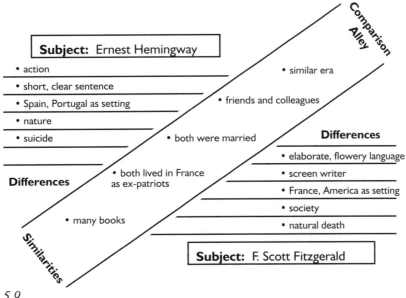

Figure 5.9

STARBURST
All Points Covered

Use the 5 points of the star to develop 5 different perspectives on a topic.

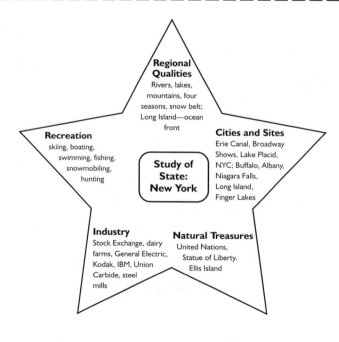

Regional Qualities
Rivers, lakes, mountains, four seasons, snow belt; Long Island—ocean front

Recreation
skiing, boating, swimming, fishing, snowmobiling, hunting

Study of State: New York

Cities and Sites
Erie Canal, Broadway Shows, Lake Placid, NYC; Buffalo, Albany, Niagara Falls, Long Island, Finger Lakes

Industry
Stock Exchange, dairy farms, General Electric, Kodak, IBM, Union Carbide, steel mills

Natural Treasures
United Nations, Statue of Liberty. Ellis Island

Figure 5.10

THE FUNNEL
Synthesizing Ideas

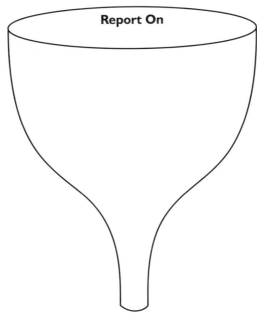

Report On

Narrowed Focus

Gradually reduce the original ideas into a creative synthesis of understanding.

- -

Report On

People, places, events, outcomes

People: Paul Revere, Red Coats, colonists

Places: Lexington and Concord, Battle of Bunker Hill, Philadelphia Conference

Events: Boston Tea Party, Declaration of Independence

Outcomes: Separation from Great Britain; U.S. Constitution; Bill of Rights; separation of church and state

Figure 5.11

Narrowed Focus Constitution: Bill of Rights

CHAIN OF EVENTS
Sequencing

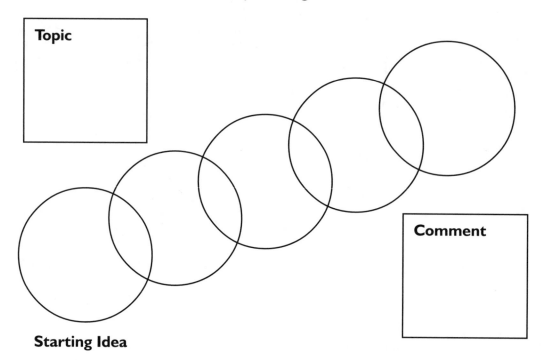

Topic

Comment

Starting Idea

Develop a sequence of events that depicts a picture from beginning to end.

- -

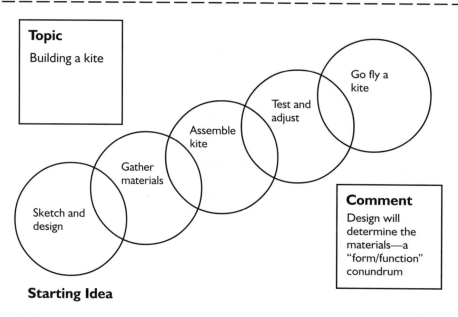

Topic
Building a kite

Sketch and design

Gather materials

Assemble kite

Test and adjust

Go fly a kite

Comment
Design will determine the materials—a "form/function" conundrum

Starting Idea

Figure 5.12

THE PUZZLER
Generating Questions

Topic:

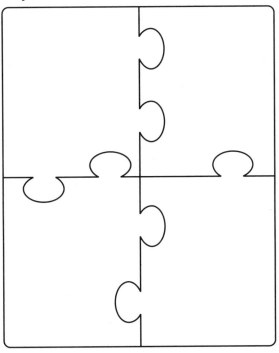

Puzzle about an idea through probing questions.

- -

Topic: Service Learning

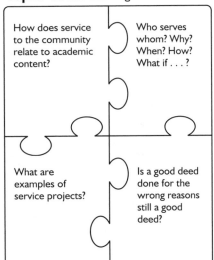

How does service to the community relate to academic content?

Who serves whom? Why? When? How? What if . . . ?

What are examples of service projects?

Is a good deed done for the wrong reasons still a good deed?

Figure 5.13

156

THE TRI PIE
Yes! No! Maybe So!

Issue

Yes!

No!

Maybe So!

Give the pros and cons of an issue, as well as a neutral position.

- -

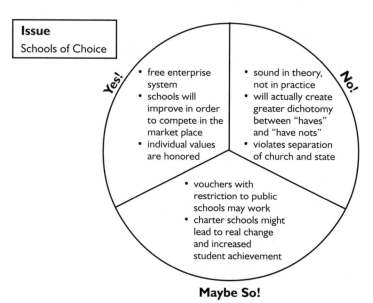

Issue
Schools of Choice

Yes!
- free enterprise system
- schools will improve in order to compete in the market place
- individual values are honored

No!
- sound in theory, not in practice
- will actually create greater dichotomy between "haves" and "have nots"
- violates separation of church and state

- vouchers with restriction to public schools may work
- charter schools might lead to real change and increased student achievement

Maybe So!

Figure 5.14

BRIDGES
Connecting Ideas

Idea

Focus

Idea

Idea

Develop two ideas and a bridge of common ground.

Idea

Parents want to do an historical journey through New England focusing on the Revolutionary War sites.

Focus

Family Vacation

Idea

New England visit to focus on history as well as fun in the sun, beaches, and carnivals this year—and next year Disnay World as well as Epcot Center and Cape Kennedy Space Center. Try to plan all vacations as educational and recreational in the future.

Idea

Kids want to go to Disney World in Florida to do all the games, rides, and shows.

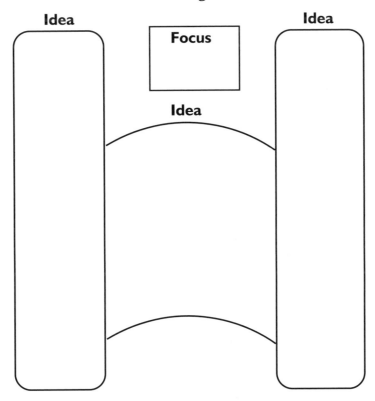

Figure 5.15

SkyLight Training and Publishing, Inc.

STAIR STEPS
Plotting a Course

Goal

Climb the stair steps to move toward a goal.
Begin with the first step and proceed to the final stages.

- -

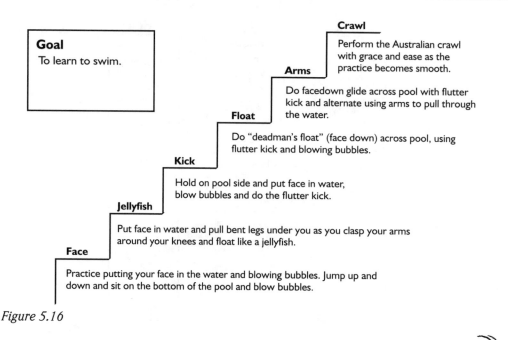

Goal
To learn to swim.

Crawl
Perform the Australian crawl with grace and ease as the practice becomes smooth.

Arms
Do facedown glide across pool with flutter kick and alternate using arms to pull through the water.

Float
Do "deadman's float" (face down) across pool, using flutter kick and blowing bubbles.

Kick
Hold on pool side and put face in water, blow bubbles and do the flutter kick.

Jellyfish
Put face in water and pull bent legs under you as you clasp your arms around your knees and float like a jellyfish.

Face
Practice putting your face in the water and blowing bubbles. Jump up and down and sit on the bottom of the pool and blow bubbles.

Figure 5.16

MIND WIND
Elaborating Ideas

Bigger Idea

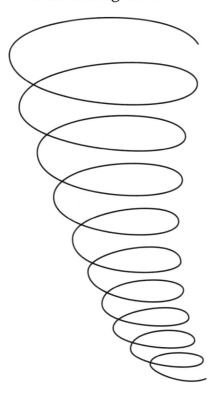

Smaller Idea

Take the smallest of ideas and let it unwind and expand into a bigger and better idea.

- -

Bigger Idea

Synthesis: Pond life is a microcosm of the life cycle contained in an ecosystem. It tells the whole story.

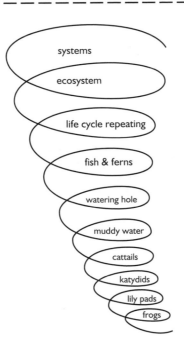

systems

ecosystem

life cycle repeating

fish & ferns

watering hole

muddy water

cattails

katydids

lily pads

frogs

Smaller Idea

Pond Life

Figure 5.17

SkyLight Training and Publishing, Inc.

160

BRAIN DROPS
Generate Ideas

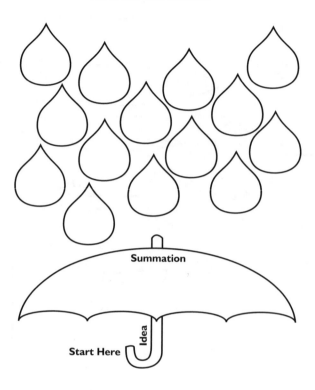

Summation

Start Here Idea

Generate ideas in the brain drops and capture the essence of the brainstorm by writing in the umbrella.

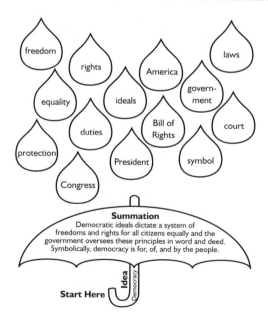

freedom

rights

America

laws

equality

ideals

govern-ment

duties

Bill of Rights

court

protection

President

symbol

Congress

Summation
Democratic ideals dictate a system of freedoms and rights for all citizens equally and the government oversees these principles in word and deed. Symbolically, democracy is for, of, and by the people.

Start Here Idea Democracy

Figure 5.18

GO TO YOUR CORNERS
Pros & Cons

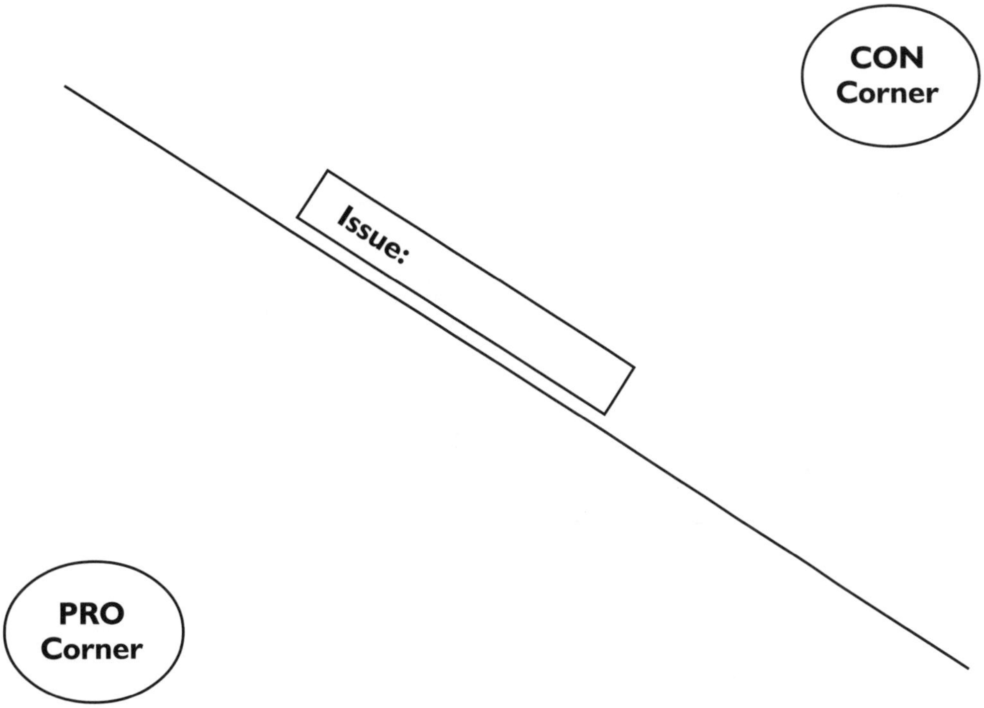

CON Corner

Issue:

PRO Corner

Develop the pros and cons of an idea by writing not fighting it out . . . go to your corners.

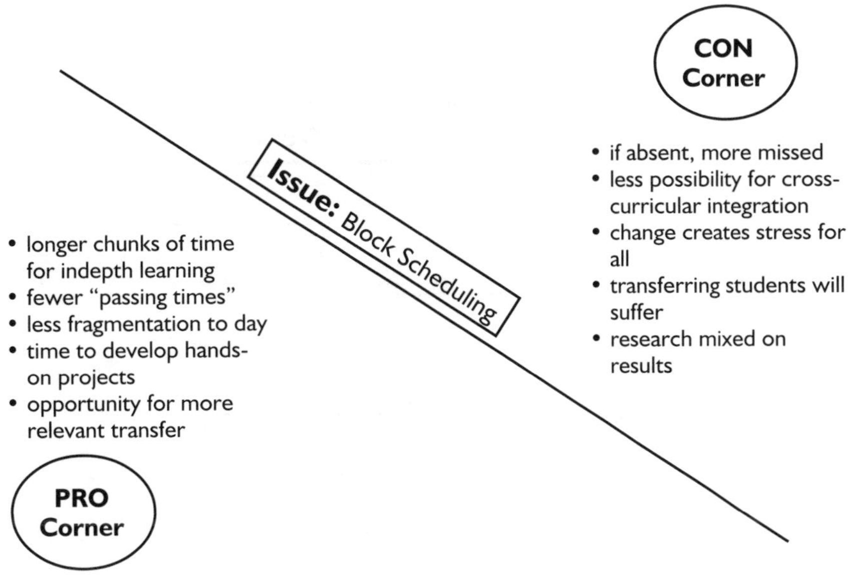

- -

CON Corner

- if absent, more missed
- less possibility for cross-curricular integration
- change creates stress for all
- transferring students will suffer
- research mixed on results

Issue: Block Scheduling

- longer chunks of time for indepth learning
- fewer "passing times"
- less fragmentation to day
- time to develop hands-on projects
- opportunity for more relevant transfer

PRO Corner

Figure 5.19

DROP DOWN MENU
Generating Options

> **Task or Goal:**

> **Menu of Options**

> _____

> _____

> _____

> _____

> _____

> _____

> _____

- -

> **Task or Goal:** Read a biography and present vital information to others in the class.

> **Menu of Presentation Options**

> Puppet Show Presentation

> Quotations on Tape

> Comic Strip

> Role Play

> Video Program

> Interview Format

> Multimedia Presentation

Figure 5.20

SkyLight Training and Publishing, Inc.

VENN

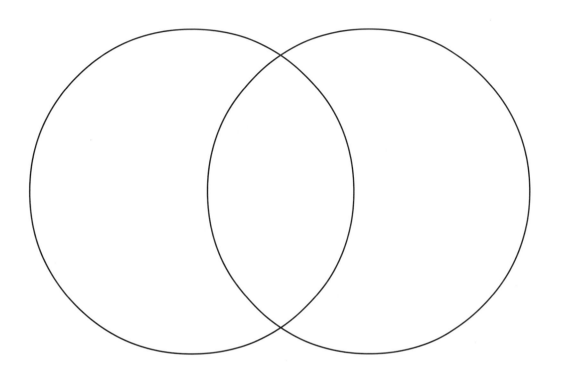

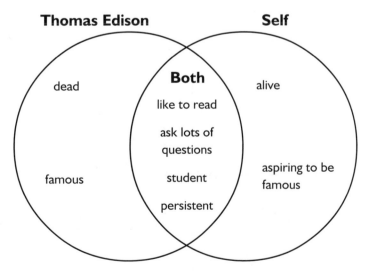

Thomas Edison   **Self**

dead

Both

like to read

ask lots of questions

alive

famous

student

persistent

aspiring to be famous

From this, students can extrapolate an essay that compares likenesses and contrasts differences.

Figure 5.21

WEB

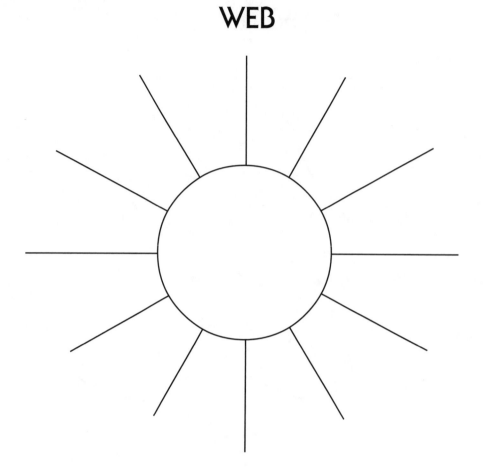

Subject: Volcanoes

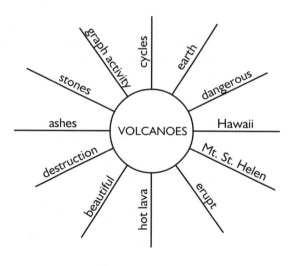

Figure 5.22

FLOW CHART

Problem:

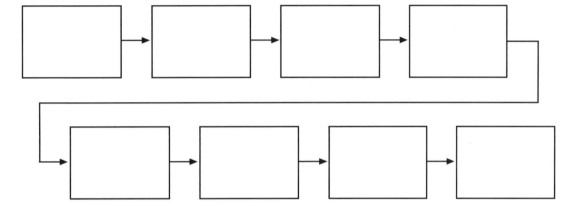

Problem: How to make a peanut butter & jelly sandwich.

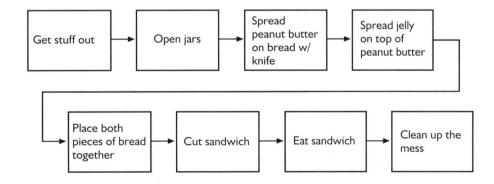

Figure 5.23

RIGHT ANGLE

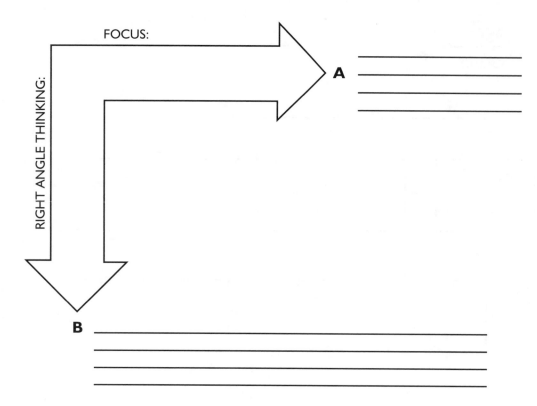

FOCUS:

RIGHT ANGLE THINKING:

A

B

- -

Leonardo da Vinci

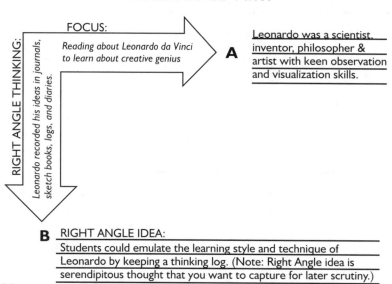

FOCUS:

RIGHT ANGLE THINKING:

Reading about Leonardo da Vinci to learn about creative genius

Leonardo recorded his ideas in journals, sketch books, logs, and diaries.

A Leonardo was a scientist, inventor, philosopher & artist with keen observation and visualization skills.

B RIGHT ANGLE IDEA:
Students could emulate the learning style and technique of Leonardo by keeping a thinking log. (Note: Right Angle idea is serendipitous thought that you want to capture for later scrutiny.)

Figure 5.24

continued from page 146

jacket. This is an example of a concrete paradox in which the vest on the bottom layer is able to be taken off without disturbing the coat on the top layer.

Afterward, have each group create Mobius strips by making a loop from a strip of paper and putting one twist in the paper before fastening the ends of the loop. Encourage investigations and comparisons of the vest exercise and the Mobius strips and introduce the concept of paradox.

Representational

Present a number of optical illusions to students and help them adjust to both perspectives of the optical illusions. Discuss the relationship to paradox and ambiguity, using the bridges graphic (see Figure 5.15). Ask why paradox and ambiguity might be relevant. Lead students to the idea of divergence and lack of closure to something in life.

Abstract

Lead students into an investigation of oxymorons and what is called compressed conflicts. Have them use the mind wind graphic organizer (see Figure 5.17) and brainstorm a spiral of phrases such as "silent shouts," "peaceful war," and "cold warmth."

Brainstorms
(APPLICATION)

Apply the concept of paradox and ambiguity appropriately to the classroom, incorporating any of the above experiences, and then relate paradox to literature or social studies or in ways that are meaningful to the curriculum.

Braindrain
(REFLECTION)

Reflect using the puzzler graphic and place these statements in each of the pieces as students think about paradox and ambiguity: Is a good deed done for the wrong reasons still a good deed? Is an unanswered prayer a no? Think about how the group work helped in the lesson. Compare the two graphic organizers that were used in the lesson (bridges and mind wind).

Brainwave
(THEME)

Experiential Learning

From the other perspective of interaction, experiential learning is the term used for immersion in the unit of study. The one immersed in the experience is the one learning from the experience. For example, if a teacher wants to teach students how to use a computer but demonstrates all the skills, how much will the students learn? The students probably won't really start to figure things out until they put their hands on the keyboard.

Experiencing the learning as authentically as possible stimulates the brain activity that leads to deep understanding. If students are invited instructionally, to use multiple ways of knowing about an idea with their many intelligences, they are more likely to grasp the idea with real under-standing. So, too, if they are exposed to integrated units in which ideas are connected under an umbrella theme or are interrelated through a problem base or a case study, then the learning is facilitated in connected ways.

In terms of the experiential learning advocated by Dewey (1933), the two areas of concern fall into experiencing the learning through the multiple intelligences (Gardner 1983) and experiencing the learning in the coherent and connected ways through integrated curriculum models (Fogarty 1991). The multiple intelligences theory offers sound instructional practice, while integrated, authentic learning provides holistic curricular models. Thus, in the discussion on structuring interaction with thinking, the reader is exposed to multiple ideas for students to become thoroughly engaged in the learning in ways that are very brain compatible.

Brainwise
(STATEMENTS)

I hear and I forget, I see and I remember, I do and I understand.

It's not how smart you are, but how you are smart.

The one who is immersed in the experience is the one who is learning.

SkyLight Training and Publishing, Inc.

Braindrops
(STRATEGIES)

Experiential learning is integrally related to the use of multiple intelligences and the incorporation of integrated curricular models.

The multiple intelligences approach is a natural way to involve all the learners holistically in the moment, and integrating the curriculum fosters an immersion approach to an idea either through umbrella themes or threaded ideas.

Multiple intelligences comprise different intelligences including the verbal and visual intelligence, the mathematical and musical, the bodily and the naturalist, the interpersonal and the intrapersonal. Integrated curriculum models projects and case studies. Figure 5.25 outlines different strategies for incorporating experiential learning.

Experiential Learning Strategies

Multiple Intelligences

- Visual/Spatial
- Verbal/Linguistic
- Logical/Mathematical
- Musical/Rhythmic

- Bodily/Kinesthetic
- Interpersonal
- Intrapersonal
- Naturalist

Integrated Curriculum

- Themes
- Problem-Based Learning
- Projects
- Case Studies

Figure 5.25

Multiple Intelligences—MI

While Gardner's multiple intelligences theory first appeared in 1983, its impact in the schools today is reaching new heights. Interestingly, the idea of multiple intelligences provides a natural framework for instruction, curriculum, and assessment decisions. Learners have unique profiles of intelligences and while they are endowed with some bit of intelligence in the many identified areas, they have peaks and valleys in their profile. They are, indeed, jagged profiles.

More specifically, Gardner identifies areas of brain processing that he labels intelligences (see Figure 5.26). These include the visual/spatial and verbal/linguistic intelligences, the logical/mathematical and musical/rhythmic intelligences, the bodily/kinesthetic intelligence, the interpersonal and intrapersonal intelligences, and the naturalist intelligence. A closer look at the intelligences reveals a literacy in each intelligence that fosters problem solving and production. In fact, the intelligences are defined as such by Gardner (1983).

The Brain and Multiple Intelligences

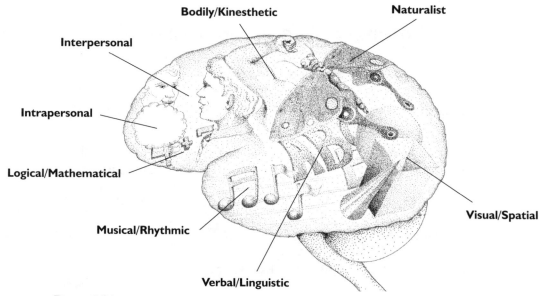

Figure 5.26

Armed with this theory of multiple intelligences, the brain-compatible classroom becomes a laboratory for experimenting with the many ways of knowing and expressing what one knows. The goal is not to teach a lesson in several different ways, although that may be a way to start, but to design learning in authentic ways that naturally tap into the various intelligences. By utilizing the multiple intelligences, the profile becomes strengthened and more balanced; the intelligences work as a complex ecosystem (see Figure 5.27). Thus, it seems much more prudent to engage a choir of intelligences rather than to artificially engage one.

SkyLight Training and Publishing, Inc.

Intelligences Working Together Like an Ecosystem

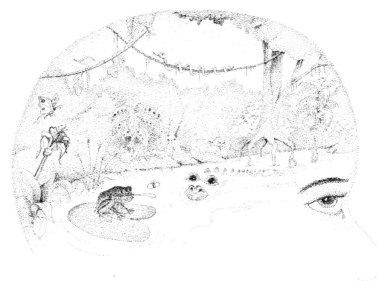

Figure 5.27

For example, when engaged in essay writing, students tap into the verbal/ linguistic intelligence, of course, but they must also use their logical/math- ematical intelligence to organize their thinking and their visual/spatial intelli- gence to format and design the final product. When planning a dramatic play, students use the bodily/kinesthetic and the verbal/linguistic intelligences for acting, the visual/spatial intelligence for the scenery, the musical/rhythmic intelligence for accompanying sound or music, the interpersonal intelligence for working with other actors and crew, and even the intrapersonal intelli- gence in taking on the roles of their characters. In short, when curriculum and instruction are designed with complexity and rigor, many of the intelli- gences come into play. This is the power of using multiple intelligences as tools in the classroom.

To introduce multiple intelligences more fully or to awaken ideas about intelligences that one might already know, the following definitions and examples are given. The applications for the creative teacher who knows about multiple intelligences are unending.

VISUAL/SPATIAL INTELLIGENCE

This intelligence comprises ones abilities to visually depict and appreciate information and ideas. The skills of the visual intelligence are found in imag- ining, visualizing, and seeing in the mind's eye. Visual representations such as maps, drawings, paintings, cartoons, architectural blueprints, film, and video are the mediums that tap the visual intelligence.

VERBAL/LINGUISTIC INTELLIGENCE

Embedded in this intelligence is the gift of language and literacy. Found in the skills of reading, writing, speaking, and listening, the print-rich environment of books, magazines, newspapers, poetry, essays, as well as speeches, dialogues, and conversation are ways that tap this vital intelligence.

LOGICAL/MATHEMATICAL INTELLIGENCE

The logical/mathematical intelligence houses the abilities to reason and think in abstractions. This intelligence is served through the skills of debating, calculating, computing, and concluding. This intelligence is tapped through mathematical problem solving, logical arguments and justifications, as well as through theory, principle, and proof.

MUSICAL/RHYTHMIC INTELLIGENCE

The musical/rhythmic intelligence gives one the sense of melody, rhythm, and rhyme. It lets one feel the beat of the music. This is the intelligence that moves people emotionally through the sound of songs and symphonies. While vocal and instrumental performance comprise this intelligence, exposure to and appreciation of music, while not performances, also tap this intelligence.

BODILY/KINESTHETIC INTELLIGENCE

The bodily/kinesthetic intelligence is manifested in the muscle memory of the body. The skills of the athlete and the dancer are expressed in this intelligence, as are the talents of the craftsperson, the carpenter, and the car mechanic. To tap this intelligence, hands-on learning, math manipulatives, labs, and practicums are avenues to pursue.

INTERPERSONAL INTELLIGENCE

The charismatic leader, the sympathetic counselor, and empathic social worker epitomize the interrelational character of this intelligence. The skills of caring, comforting, collaborating, and communicating bring this intelligence into being. Small and large group activities, team tasks, and partner work awaken and develop this intelligence.

INTRAPERSONAL INTELLIGENCE

The intelligence named the intrapersonal intelligence is found in the inner nature and soul of the person. It is the inner thought—the reflective self. The skills of the intrapersonal intelligence are seen in the abilities to be self-aware, self-regulating, and self-assessing. Learning logs, response journals, goal setting, and personal portfolios are tools of the trade to tap this intelligence.

NATURALIST INTELLIGENCE

The intelligence of the naturalist can be realized in the abilities to discern the differences in species of flora and fauna, in the ability to understand the interrelatedness of things in nature, and in the survival instincts all people possess. The skills of the naturalist lie in the realm of knowing about and being able to classify forms of wildlife, including all the various species of plants and animals. The skills of the naturalist are tapped through nature walks and rooms filled with living organisms such as plants and flowers, animals, rocks and fossils, and seashells.

Integrated Curriculum—IC

The brain seeks connections, patterns, and chunks of information that fit together (Caine and Caine 1991). By structuring learning around authentic designs such as projects, problems, and real-life dilemmas, the connectedness and relevance are inherent in the learning. When students are building a model, solving the problems that accompany a mock election, or deliberating about the ethics of the media, the learning is both purposeful and meaningful. The learning is also contextual, tying the ideas together within the fabric of the key understandings (Fogarty 1993).

Often the projects and events that are considered extracurricular are the authentic kinds of experiences that integrate the skills and concepts from within and across the disciplines. Publishing a school newspaper, developing the yearbook, producing the musical or the school play, orchestrating a spaghetti dinner as a fund-raiser, or synchronizing the marching band for the football game—these are the experiences that pull the threads of learning together.

Now, that is not to say that all learning must be integrated or interdisciplinary in nature. In fact, the opposite is probably closer to the ideal. Learning that is discrete within a discipline develops the literacy (and the lingo) of the discipline in a pure way; a way that is inherent to the particular rigors and expertise of the discipline. For example, to learn to conduct a scientific investigation through the time-honored techniques of the scientific method is to learn science as a scientist. To study genre through the treasured literature of the ages is to learn literature in the style of the classicists. To learn computer literacy such as multimedia presentations in the manner of the technology wizards is to learn in the context of a computer programmer.

Yet, to learn within the discipline and not to apply the learning to contexts of real-life situations is to short-circuit the process. The glory and the real value of an integrated curriculum are to give relevance and purpose to the skill and concept of learning that occurs within the realms of the disciplines as we know them. Thematic units, authentic projects, case studies, and problems that replicate real life lend credence to the disparate skills and concepts learned within the parameters of a discipline.

When teachers move the learning into more integrated contexts, the brain is better able to chunk the information, see like patterns, and link ideas to one another. Thus, it is imperative in the brain-compatible classroom to strive for both learning within the discipline and application beyond the discipline—integrated and connected to real-life events. The discussion that follows suggests four types of integrated applications: themes, problems, projects, and cases. While there are many more models that foster relevant, purposeful learning, these serve to illustrate the idea.

THEMES

To use an umbrella theme (Fogarty and Stoehr 1995) to cover overlapping skills and concepts from various content is both appropriate for and invitational to student learning. The big ideas that override different content provide obvious, visible, and known connections from one subject area to another. These ideas become recursive in the learning and create strong neural pathways (see chapter 1).

The idea of a tapestry and the overarching impact it has for the many disciplines offers a good metaphor. Some examples are the tapestry of the novel, painting, investigation, culture; the tapestry of geometry, algebraic notation, or computation; the tapestry of nature or research; or the tapestry of a foreign language. The idea of tapestry, in its broadest sense, provides an integrative theme for learning that has great appeal to students of any age.

To use thematic instruction, teachers brainstorm a number of themes, select one to use, and then develop essential questions that provide depth in the thematic investigations. If activities align to targeted goals, the theme develops naturally. Themes should change often enough to keep students motivated and energized.

PROBLEM-BASED LEARNING

Problems provide great fodder for the brain. They stimulate brain activity in various ways. The brain becomes a pattern-seeking, sense-making, connection-finding mechanism, functioning efficiently and effectively as it tries to bring harmony to the dissonance it is sensing. The more complex the problem, the more complex the brain activity becomes. In fact, problem solving relates to the idea discussed earlier in the text about challenge and how challenge engages the intellect (see chapter 3).

An emerging model for the classroom comes from the medical model of interns, in which the problem of the patient is presented and the students, with guidance from the experts, work to diagnose and prescribe. Now, the model that is evolving in the schools takes a slightly different form (Fogarty 1997). Students are presented with an open-ended situation called an ill-structured problem. Then, using their questioning skills and their research skills, they attempt to zero in on the primary problem, gather the necessary data, generate alternatives, and recommend a viable solution. The key to this authentic learning model is that the students take on the role of one of the stakeholders; therefore, they tend to become invested in the solution. In addition, the goals of the problem-based unit are aligned to the goals of the class, so the experience has a definite academic plan.

A specific example of a problem-based learning unit is one in which the students tackle the graffiti problem in the neighborhood surrounding the school grounds. They take on the roles of citizens who own property in the area and live in the neighborhood. Their responsibilities as problem solvers are to gather the data, to compile ideas, and to recommend action to the local citizenry. Naturally, their investigation leads them to local news articles and media reports, various civic groups, and interviews with the people in the neighborhoods. The authenticity of the learning is based in the problem, thus, problem-based learning.

To develop problem-based learning scenarios, teachers often collaborate and collect a stock of possible situations. Then, each teacher or teacher team revises and refines the problem scenarios appropriate to academic goals and the ages and stages of the learners involved. The problem-based unit unfolds with the students taking the lead. The learner, of course, is monitored by the teacher, and minilessons or instructional interludes occur as necessary.

PROJECTS

As most teachers know, projects of any sort garner the intense interest and earnest efforts of students. Students love projects because they love to dig in and mess around and figure things out. They can become as interested in constructing a kite as they are in creating scenery for a play. They have as much energy for inventing electrical wizardry as they do for reenacting events in history.

Student projects are unlimited in number, type, and scope. Projects are compelling to students, the learning is natural, and they are easily integrated with the various aspects of the instruction, curriculum, and assessment cycle (Berman 1997).

For example, a project can serve to kick off a unit of study: Students make models of pyramids as they begin their study of Egypt. Projects can become the heart of the unit of study: Students incorporate simple machines in their working models of dragons. Or, projects can be used to culminate a unit: Student teams demonstrate their solar energy cars as part of their performance assessment for the science unit on alternative sources of energy.

To incorporate more projects into the learning is goal of the brain-compatible classroom. Teachers working in grade level or department teams or interdisciplinary clusters can easily find appropriate projects that make the learning more genuine for students.

CASE STUDIES

The study of a specific case scenario offers a viable curricular model similar to problem-based learning. The case study begins with a problematic situation, which, in this instance, is referred to as a dilemma. In fact, the case study model taps into the moral intelligence that Coles (1997) speaks of. In the case study approach, students are presented a sticky situation and through questioning, in the vein of Socratic dialogue, their goal is to unravel the situation. In the rigor of the questioning and dialogue that ensues, students are led to examine their own values and beliefs.

Case studies are written around moral and ethical issues such as telling the truth and caring for and respecting elders. With older students, issues such as gay rights, human rights, or the medical dilemma of life-support systems are possible. In all of these cases, the research, the discussions, and the related activities are aligned to predetermined goals of the curriculum.

To actually use the case study model in the classroom, teachers find that if they write the cases themselves, key academic areas are more easily targeted. For example, one teacher used the issue of censorship and created a case around censorship on television. The student research, however, stretched into the realm of the V-chip and even censorship on the Internet, which was also a current concern to the Board of Education. The teacher was then able to tie into the class the media unit and technology research.

In this way, the teacher determines the issues and can readily design related activities to fuel in-depth discussions and debriefing sessions following the case study. As in other authentic models, learning is compelling for students. They can barely stop talking about the issues because they are relevant. Naturally, all sorts of reading and writing as well as communications activities and student-generated projects result.

Brainworks
(ACTIVITIES)

CURRICULUM CORNERS

Post signs on the four different walls of the room: THEMES, PROJECTS, PROBLEMS, CASE STUDIES. Then, allow students to form small groups next to one of the charts to form a go-to-your-corners graphic. Have students create appropriate lists for each chart: possible themes, projects, problems, or issues for cases.

Once the lists are developed, have the teams select one idea from their lists to work with. Let groups proceed accordingly:

Themes: Develop essential questions
Problems: Describe problem scenario and stakeholder role
Projects: Develop procedures and guidelines
Case Studies: Write a case study around the selected issue

Then, using the multiple intelligences grid in Figure 5.28, have each group brainstorm appropriate activities. As the grid fills up with ideas, designate specific challenging learning experiences as possible assessment pieces.

For example, identify items for a student portfolio and for student performance assessment.

Brainstorm
(APPLICATION)

Develop a multiple intelligences approach to an active learning lesson using the web (see Figure 5.29).

To apply the ideas about experiential learning, select one of the curriculum models and create a personally relevant grid, working with one other teacher who teaches in a similar situation.

Braindrain
(REFLECTION)

Reflect on the ideas of multiple intelligences or integrated curriculum by using the pro and con approach of the go-to-your-corners graphic.

WAYS TO EXPERIENCE LEARNING

Verbal	Visual	Logical	Musical	Interpersonal	Intrapersonal	Bodily	Naturalist									

Figure 5.28   SkyLight Training and Publishing, Inc.

WEB

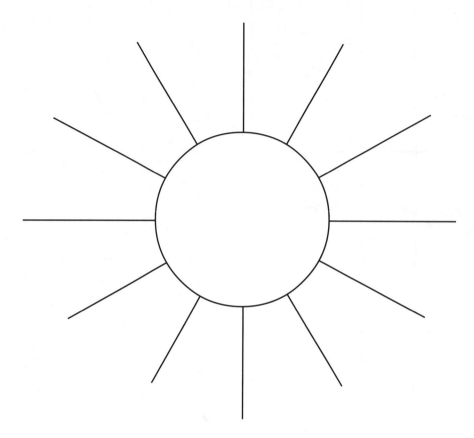

MI Web

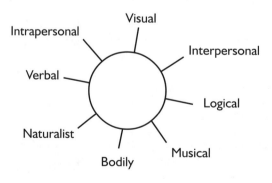

Figure 5.29

THINKING *about* THINKING

Neurons that fire together wire together.

—PAT WOLFE

KEY

Brainwave: Theme
Big idea that relates to the brain research and/or learning theory

Brainwise: Statements
Quips, statements, or memorable sayings about the brain and learning

Braindrops: Strategies
Strategies, tools, and techniques that help implement instructional methods based on brain research and the learning theory

Brainworks: Activities
Activities or learning experiences for the reader (or workshop participant) to do and to actively think about the presented information

Brainstorms: Application
Personally relevant transfer by reader or workshop participant to tailor for immediate use

Braindrain: Reflection
Reflection and thought about the ideas and processes

SkyLight Training and Publishing, Inc.

CHAPTER 6

THINKING
about
THINKING

Metacognitive reflection, or the mind watching itself, is essential to the learning process. In the metacognitive moment, the learner plans, monitors, and evaluates his or her own thinking and learning. The reflection is the pause in the act of learning that deepens understanding and gives meaning to the learning. In metacognitive processing, or reflecting, the learner is first self-aware and second self-regulatory. The mature learner knows that to really know, to fully comprehend something, is a moment when the learner is aware of what he or she is learning and how well he or she is learning it. This awareness and control over one's thinking and learning is the key to learning that has breadth and depth for future use.

Implied in the realm of metacognition, or the moments of thinking about one's thinking, there are two arenas to consider. One is in the reflection of the learning and the other is in the assessment of that learning. Both are of utmost importance in the brain-compatible classroom. For in the reflection, the mind makes meaning of the learning and is then able to generalize the learning for transfer to similar and novel situations. In the assessment of the learning, there are summative measures and dynamic data that both lend credence to the extent and quality of the learning. An integral part of the assessment is in the self-assessing techniques of the student. This involves an awareness and control over one's own learning and is extremely metacognitive in nature.

Both the reflective phase and the assessment phase of metacognitive process are addressed in this final section of the four-corner framework for brain-compatible classrooms. The discussion about reflection covers making meaning of the learning and transferring the learning to relevant applications. From the perspective of assessments, the discussion compares and contrasts the traditional measures to dynamic, fluid assessments.

#7

Brainwave
(THEME)

Reflection

The mind is like a mirror that reflects images of the learning for a somewhat silent and prolonged look. The reflection sometimes gives the mind quite an accurate image and other times the reflection is distorted by emotional baggage or other forms of interference. Yet, without the benefit of reflection, much of the initial learning could be lost. The reflection gives students time to scrutinize, observe, and question. In the reflective phase of learning, the mind sorts and synthesizes, rearranges and reconnects. This is when transfer takes place. This is the phase of the learning cycle that moves inert knowledge to relevant application.

In this reflective phase the mind literally rewires itself based on the new experiences and the new learnings. This rewiring of the neurons through new dendrite connections is the way the brain links new ideas to other ideas already in the brain. These linkings are, in essence, the way the brain makes meaning of the information for future transfer, application, and purposeful use. Therefore, "Neurons that fire together wire together" (Wolfe 1996).

Brainwise
(STATEMENTS)

The human mind, once stretched to a new idea, never goes back to its original dimensions.

An intellectual is someone whose mind watches itself. —CAMUS

Our rewards come not from having brains but in using them.

Braindrops
(STRATEGIES)

This discussion delineates four aspects of the meaning-making processes in the mind and other elements that lead to transfer of learning (see Figure 6.1). In particular, the areas that are investigated for making meaning are 1) understanding that making meaning is inextricably linked to personal relevance, 2) constructing knowledge, 3) fostering deep understanding, and 4) extrapolating generalizations. The transfer of learning specifically covers strategies to promote transfer, such as cognitive mediation, metacognitive reflection, and application. The different levels of transfer are outlined as well as ways to enhance transfer.

Reflection Strategies

Making Meaning

- Personal Relevance
- Knowledge Construction
- Deep Understanding
- Generalizations

Transfer of Learning

- Cognitive Mediation
- Metacognitive Reflection
- Application
- Transfer Levels
- Enhancing Transfer

Figure 6.1

SkyLight Training and Publishing, Inc.

Making Meaning

The idea of making meaning is at the heart of the constructivist theory, which basically states that learning is constructed in the mind of the learner. In this sense, learners take information into their own schemata or mental organizational system and try to make sense of it by fitting the new information into an existing chunk or pattern. When the learning has personal relevance, knowledge is constructed more easily, generalizable ideas are generated, and deep understanding results.

In the brain-compatible classroom, learners are given opportunities to internalize ideas and make meaning in their own time and in their own way.

PERSONAL RELEVANCE

For the brain to attend to an idea—to instantly decide that it wants to hold onto the information flowing through the neural pathways at the rate of 250 miles per hour—the information has to have an emotional hook, personal relevance, or discernible meaning.

The emotional hook is easy. The limbic system automatically enacts (see chapter 1), and the hook is in. The link to personal relevance is sometimes less obvious. The idea may at first seem to have no personal connection, but then a mere glimpse of something makes the needed connection. For example, a person reads a headline in the paper about a child who is missing from a neighboring town. At first, this person passes over the article but then notices a familiar word, such as the name of the town. Then he or she reads on because the information now has a relevant link.

To foster neural linking in the brain and to label the information "relevant," as a signal to the brain to pay attention, teachers should try to make an explicit statement about why the students need to take notice, should elicit possible uses for an idea from the students themselves, or should just link someone's name to an idea and awaken the brain to an important incoming thought.

KNOWLEDGE CONSTRUCTION

The most elemental stage of learning is acquiring a knowledge base. In the early learning stages of any number of situations, what do people learn first? The answer is vocabulary—words that allow people to identify things and talk about them. This is true of a basic writing class, French I, beginning computing, general science, or even a beginners ski class.

Once students are empowered with the language, the knowledge base grows around the terminology. Yes, the brain literally grows dendrites that connect around a particular set of neurons that are becoming more interconnected. For example, as one is learning about online services on the Internet, words and phrases such as e-mail, sign on, Web site, home page, server, Netscape, chat room, and WebCrawler are logged into the knowledge base. This vocabulary allows the learner to continue to talk and read about online research and related issues. Without the initial knowledge base, the learning is short-circuited because there is nothing to attach the learning to.

To develop a knowledge base, deductive approaches such as direct instruction, mentoring models, coaching, and internships are expedient ways to learn the initial information. In addition, more natural, inductive methods such as inquiry learning, hands-on discovery learning, and group investigations can provide an initial layer of knowledge to build on.

DEEP UNDERSTANDING

To teach for deep understanding is to teach with rigor and vigor, over time. Deep understanding seldom happens fast. It is a layering process that builds idea upon idea, concept upon concept, skill upon skill. To achieve deep understanding, one goes beyond a genuine knowledge base. Deep understanding requires factual information, relevant associations, and conscious thought about its meaning and the implications of that meaning.

Deep understanding occurs only when students know enough about something to know that they, in fact, know very little. The paradox is that a little knowledge opens the eyes to the larger field of study. That's why the saying, A little knowledge is dangerous, was formed. When a student has superficial information or surface knowledge without the deep understanding to ground the learning, action may be taken with little insight or forethought for implications and consequences of the action.

To teach for deep understanding, a major revolution in thinking about curriculum must occur. The concept of curriculum coverage must be replaced with the idea of curriculum priorities. Schools cannot continue the race to cover the content in every subject area. There is simply too much content to cover. Instead, the content of every discipline must be examined for the essential conceptual learnings. Once the curricular priorities are set, skillful, authentic designs, such as problem-based learning and case studies are implemented to foster deep understanding for long-term learning.

GENERALIZATIONS

One of the foremost reflective strategies for making meaning is in the ability to generalize the learning. Through generalizations, principles are founded and concepts are organized and affirmed. Ideas move from the concrete to the abstract, and generalizable bits of information are linked appropriately in a spectrum of related realms. An illustration of the power of generalizations in making meaning of new information is learning about weather and all the data and information that is compiled to make tomorrow's forecast. From generalizations about recurring cloud patterns, the flow of the jet stream, or the impact the barometric pressure has on the weather, accurate forecasts are formed.

To take the generalizations a step further, if one extrapolates the process for predicting the weather, a similar process may lead to other kinds of predictions that are also accurate. For instance, if gathering data from multiple sources, searching for patterns of reliability, and tracking trends over a period of time lead to accurate forecasts in weather, perhaps appropriate procedures coupled with a similar process might lead to accurate predictions for the stock market. The ability to generalize, although simplified greatly in this brief discussion, is a primary strategy for reflecting on learning and for making meaning of the learning.

One thing that teachers can do to foster the skill of generalizing is ask three questions: Have you ever seen anything like this before? How does this connect to something else you know? How might you use this idea, again? When the teacher pushes for connections to prior knowledge and to future application, the learner is forced to find the big idea to the generalizable idea in the learning.

Transfer of Learning

All learning is for transfer. The goal of all learning is to make information portable, so the learning travels with the learner to new locations. In the new locations the learning is transferred and applied in novel, interesting, and innovative ways. This is the phenomenon referred to as the transfer of learning. Think of some learning that carried from one situation to the next. Perhaps it was something learned about managing a classroom the first year of teaching. Notice how some of the early learnings are still being implemented today.

But, how is transfer fostered? How can teachers promote the transfer of learning so it moves from one context to another? What are the elusive elements of transfer that need explicit attention? In the ensuing discussion, transfer of learning is related to the brain-compatible classroom as a critical strategy that enhances learning—not for a test, but a for a lifetime. Strategies that promote this kind of transfer of learning are cognitive mediation, metacognitive reflection, and direct application. Cognitive mediation is the teacher leading the students to self-reflection, or thinking about their own thinking; metacognitive reflection is student-initiated self-reflection; and direct application is learner awareness of the self-reflective process through purposeful use.

As part of the repertoire of strategies to promote transfer are the various levels of transfer and ways to enhance transfer. Further discussion illustrates this idea in more detail.

COGNITIVE MEDIATION

The concept of cognitive mediation (Feuerstein 1980) means that learning can be mediated or facilitated; that human intervention in the learning, at the right time and in the right way, can help the learner in the learning process. In fact, cognitive mediation not only facilitates the learning, but also deepens the learning for future transfer and use. It is explicit intervention by the teacher to guide students' thinking and reflection. In brief, cognitive mediation occurs when the teacher mediates the learning.

The principles of cognitive mediation (Feuerstein 1980) involve several, interrelated components. These critical elements are intentionality and reciprocity, meaning, and transcendence. A closer look at these terms reveals insight into the transfer process.

To have intentionality, the teacher deliberately guides the learning in a specific direction, and reciprocity occurs when there is an indication that the learner is receptive to the mediation or guided learning. To have meaning, the mediator signifies the significance and purpose of the learning and elicits an understanding of why the activity is important. Finally, to mediate for transcendence means to take the learning beyond the immediate situation and into the realm of proven principles, concepts, and strategies for use in other circumstances.

While the elements of meaning and transcendence are similar to the ideas in the section on making meaning through relevance and generalizations, in the case of cognitive mediation, the intervention is much more direct and intentional. In fact, cognitive mediation as it is represented here is explicitly designed to extract certain key learnings. The mediation goes beyond the push for finding personal relevance and seeking generalizations.

The easiest and most direct way to mediate the learning is to be clear and explicit about the purpose, elicit some response from the learners to indicate their ownership in the process, extract meaning from the learners through probing questions and personal comments, and push the transfer by getting the learners to think of opportunities to use the idea again.

METACOGNITIVE REFLECTION

To speak of transfer without speaking of metacognition would be like rowing a boat without the oars. Metacognition moves the transfer boat, and without it, the boat would be adrift at sea. In other words, metacognition, the ability to think about your own thinking, to be aware of the learning, and to control the learning, is the key to effective and skillful transfer.

An examination of metacognitive activity suggests that this is thinking beyond (meta-) the cognitive. It is thinking about, around, and outside of the cognitive focus. That is to say, the metacognitive behavior is the thinking that is done when one plans, monitors, or evaluates one's own learning. It is thinking beyond the immediate situation, similar to looking through a window at oneself and knowing what one is doing and how one is doing it.

For example, a teacher is giving a lesson on fractions. The teacher is about to finish the demonstration on the board, when she becomes aware that the students' "eyes are glazed over." They don't get it. That sudden awareness of the circumstances surrounding the actual cognitive lesson being taught, that cue that the lesson is not connecting, that is metacognitive monitoring on the part of the teacher.

Likewise, metacognitive reflection might be in the form of planning, monitoring, or evaluating the lesson. Again, the thinking is about, around, and outside of the actual teaching part. It is reflective thinking before, during, or after the action takes place. It is the time when the teacher is anticipating what might happen, what is happening, or evaluating what did happen (see Figure 6.2).

To foster the metacognitive thinking in students, planning time is built in for groups to predict what might happen, strategies are included that force

Metacognition Chart

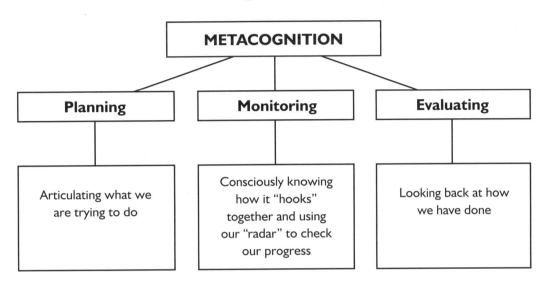

Figure 6.2

them to self-monitor their progress, and self-evaluation tools are employed to foster reflective analysis after the fact.

Swartz and Perkins (1989) elaborate on the concept of metacognition by describing four distinct levels of thinking. They begin the levels with metacognition that is tacit and move to an awareness level, then to a strategic phase, and finally to a reflective stage. Each level has a specific mode that is notable.

Tacit Level of Metacognition: The tacit level of metacognition is evidenced when a behavior is repeated because it is working. However, this level implies that there is no real awareness that the behavior is working, but it is tacit or automatic—not with conscious awareness. For example, a writer might always write at the kitchen table with the radio on in the background. It works, therefore, the writer continues but never really never analyzes the process.

Aware Level of Metacognition: To move to the level of awareness, the behavior has to be consciously noted. The learner must become aware of the behavior and think about it explicitly. If the ingredients of awareness are added to the writer from the above example, the writer now notices that she always sits at the kitchen table with the radio on in the background. She may even comment on this to someone. She is aware.

192

Strategic Level of Metacognition: At the strategic level of metacognition, the learner is not only aware of his or her specific behavior but actively strategizes to repeat the behavior. In this example, the writer is not at home, so she is not able to sit at the kitchen table. However, the writer strategically recreates the situation to resemble her "favorite" mode. The writer finds a table or desk and sets a radio nearby, thus creating a familiar atmosphere for writing.

Reflective Level of Metacognition: The reflective level of metacognitive behavior moves beyond the strategic level when there is deliberate thought about the best or easiest way to do something. The reflective level implies that there is true reflective thought guiding the action. Therefore, the writer, in this reflective model, not only sits at the kitchen table with the radio in the background but gingerly selects the "right" station. The writer reflects on the effects of the different kinds of music and chooses accordingly.

Specific tools for transfer that have classroom appeal include a questioning strategy called Mrs. Potter's questions (see Figure 6.3), and evaluation chart called the PMI (see Figure 6.4), a reflective schemata that elicits "What?" "So what?" "Now what?" (see Figure 6.5), the KWL strategy (see Figure 6.6), and learning logs (see Figure 6.7).

APPLICATION

Application, or purposeful use, is highly metacognitive because it demonstrates concrete transfer of the learning from one context to the next. The application may be implicit or explicit; some self-reflection has to occur for the transfer to take place.

The surest way to foster transfer is to create a need for immediate use. The sooner the learning is actually applied and used, the greater the chance for permanence. That is to say, when the learning is purposefully applied by the learner, the learning becomes anchored in the mind. It is attached and held in the mind within a meaningful context. Thus, the learning is likely to be placed in long-term memory.

Hopefully, the learning can be authentically used in a meaningful application, such as incorporating more adverbial phrases in a draft of writing, following a lesson on adverbs. But, even if the application is somewhat

Continued on page 198

SkyLight Training and Publishing, Inc.

MRS. POTTER'S QUESTIONS

- What were you expected to do?

- In this assignment, what did you do well?

- If you had to do this task over, what would you do differently?

- What help do you need from me?

Figure 6.3

194

PMI

Plus / Minus / Intriguing
P(+) Plus	
M(–) Minus	
I(?) Intriguing	

Figure 6.4

WHAT? SO WHAT? NOW, WHAT?

Metacognition
What?
So What?
Now What?
What Else?

Figure 6.5

KWL

Strategy Sheet		
What We **K**now	What We **W**ant to Find Out	What We Have **L**earned

Figure 6.6

LOG LEAD-INS

Lead-Ins That Promote Thinking at Higher Levels

Analysis

Compared to . . .
The best part . . .
On the positive scale . . .
An interesting part is . . .
Take a small part like . . .
A logical sequence seems to be . . .
On the negative side . . .
Similarily . . .
By contrast . . .

Synthesis

Suppose . . .
Combine . . .
Possibly . . .
Imagine . . .
Reversed . . .
What if . . .
I predict . . .
How about . . .
I wonder . . .

Evaluation

How . . .
Why . . .
It seems irrelevant that . . .
One point of view is . . .
It seems important to note . . .
The best . . .
The worst . . .
If ___ then . . .

Application

Backtracking for a minute . . .
A way to . . .
I want to . . .
A connecting idea is . . .
A movie this reminds me of is __ because . . .
If this were a book I'd title it . . .
I think this applies to . . .
Does this mean . . .

Problem Solving

I'm stuck on . . .
The best way to think about this . . .
I conclude . . .
I'm lost with . . .
I understand, but . . .
I'm concerned about. . .
My problem is . . .
A question I have is . . .

Decision Making

I disagree with ___ because . . .
I prefer ___ because . . .
If I had to choose . . .
I believe . . .
My goal is . . .
I hate . . .
One criticism is . . .
I can't decide if . . .

Lead-Ins That Promote Different Styles of Thinking

Visual Representations

Try to visualize . . .
My picture of this . . .
A diagram of this idea looks like . . .
I feel like . . .
A chart . . .
I'm ___ like ___ because . . .

Verbal Presentations

Another way of saying this is . . .
I learned . . .
I discovered . . .
A quote that seems to fit is . . .
I want to read ___ because . . .
I want to talk to ___ because . . .

Figure 6.7

SkyLight Training and Publishing, Inc.

Continued from page 192

contrived, such as a playing a game in which the adverbs are used or creating cartoons based on adverbial phrases, the application is still of value and does help to foster transfer.

TRANSFER LEVELS

Transfer extends learning, bridges the old and the new, and leads students toward relevant application across academic content and into life situations. In some cases, the transfer of learning is obvious because the learned skills seem close to the skill situation in which they are used or transferred. For example, when teaching "supermarket math" (price comparisons, making change, etc) the learning situation "hugs" the life situation. The transfer is clear. This transfer is called simple transfer.

In other instances, the learning in the school situation seems far removed or remote from the transfer across content or into life. For example, a high school student spends a great deal of time and energy staring at, memorizing, and using the periodic table. However, unless the student is destined for a scientific career in which frequent reference and deep understanding of the periodic table is essential, it is difficult for the student to feel that the learning is really useful. The high school student wonders if he or she really needs to know that Au is gold.

Most students do not "see" how this learning is useful. The transfer is complex. They miss the connection between the rigors of learning the elements and the similar rigors of visualizing, practicing, and memorizing other material. Few students note that the analytical skills used in "reading" the periodic table are similar to the critical thinking skills used in analyzing other charts or graphs. Seldom are students aware that the patterns evident in the periodic table set a model for searching for patterns in other phenomena or constructing similar matrices or grids. The transfer here is remote; it is obscure. The student needs explicit instruction in making these and other connections. In these situations, teachers can help students make relevant transfer through mediation or "bridging" strategies.

The six transfer strategies illustrated in Figures 6.8, 6.9, and 6.10 require explicit instruction with students to help them make application, in other words, to help students transfer learning.

TRANSFER OF LEARNING

Model	Illustration	Transfer Disposition	Looks Like	Sounds Like
Ollie the Head-in-the-sand Ostrich		Overlooks	Persists in writing in manuscript form rather than cursive. (New skill overlooked or avoided.)	*"I get it right on the dittos, but I forget to use punctuation When I write an essay."* (Not applying mechanical learning.)
Dan the Drilling Woodpecker		Duplicates	Plagiarism is the most obvious student artifact of duplication. (Unable to synthesize in own words.)	*"Mine is not to question why—just invert and multiply." (When dividing fractions.)* (No understanding of what she/he is doing.)
Laura the Look-alike Penguin		Replicates	"Bed to Bed" or narrative style. "He got up. He did this. He went to bed, or he was born. He did this… He died." (Student portfolio of work never varies.)	*"Paragraphing means I must have three 'indents' per page."* (Tailors into own story or essay, but paragraphs inappropriately.)
Jonathan Livingston Seagull		Integrates	Student writing essay incorporates newly learned French words. (Applying: weaving old and new.)	*"I always try to guess (predict) what's gonna happen next on TV shows."* (Connects to prior knowledge and experience; relates what's learned to personal experience.)
Cathy the Carrier Pigeon		Maps	Graphs information for a social studies report with the help of the math teacher to actually design the graphs. (Connecting to another.)	Parent-related story: *"Tina suggested we brainstorm our vacation ideas and rank them to help us decide."* (Carries new skills into life situations.)
Samantha the Soaring Eagle		Innovates	After studying flow charts for computer class student constructs a Rube Goldberg type invention. (Innovates: Invents; diverges; goes beyond and creates something novel.)	*"I took the idea of the Mr. Potato Head and created a mix and match grid of ideas for our Earth Day project."* (Generalizes ideas from experience and transfers creatively.)

Figure 6.8   SkyLight Training and Publishing, Inc.

TRANSFER STRATEGY:
MAKING CONNECTIONS WITH QUESTIONS

Overlooking

Think of an instance where the skill or strategy would be inappropriate.
"I would not use _____ when _____."

Duplicating

Think of an "opportunity passed" when you could have used the skill or strategy.
"I wish I'd known about _____ when _____ because I could've_____."

Replicating

Think of an adjustment that will make your application of ___ more relevant.
"Next time I'm gonna _____."

Integrating

Think of an analogy for the skill or strategy.
"_____ is like _____ because both_____."

Mapping

Think of an upcoming opportunity in classes to use the new idea.
"In _____, I'm gonna use _____ to help_____."

Innovating

Think of an application for a "real-life" setting.
"Outside of school, I could use_____ when_____."

Figure 6.9   SkyLight Training and Publishing, Inc.

SITUATIONAL DISPOSITIONS TOWARD TRANSFER

Does the learner

OVERLOOK: Miss appropriate opportunities; persist in former ways?

DUPLICATE: Perform the drill exactly as practiced; duplicate with no change; copy?

REPLICATE: Tailor, but apply knowledge only in similar situations; produce work that all looks alike?

INTEGRATE: Subtly combine knowledge with other ideas and situations; use information with raised consciousness?

MAP: Carry a strategy to another content and into life situations; associate?

INNOVATE: Invent; take ideas beyond the initial conception; take risks; diverge?

SIMPLE

COMPLEX

NEAR

FAR

Figure 6.10

Enhancing Transfer

Application, use, and meaningful transfer are facilitated in a distinct way. These include decontextualizing learning through generalizations, crystallizing learning for deep understanding, recontextualizing learning for purposeful use, energizing learning with active involvement, and personalizing learning for internalization.

Decontextualized Learning: What's the Big Idea?

When process instruction becomes the content of instruction, transfer is enhanced because learning is decontextualized (Feuerstein et al., 1980); skills, operations, and dispositions are easily extracted from original contexts through generalizations and a focus on the "big ideas." Learning more readily targets relevant life skills as subject matter content becomes the vehicle for learning. For example, while studying about disease and the relationship to health and wellness, students learn the critical skills of cause and effect, comparing and contrasting, and drawing conclusions. The curiosity they experience drives continued and persistent inquiry, and they gain insight into the interdependence of all things. These are all processes they can take away with them. Knowledge, facts, and information are naturally the products of this learning, but perhaps more important, the students' tools of critical thinking are honed and their habits of mind begin to take shape.

Decontextualized learning "chunks" learning into discernible patterns that reveal universal attributes. These generalizable chunks are often mediated through analogies in which the generic pattern is uncovered and analogous ideas are slotted in, thereby chunking learning for future use (Perkins & Salomon, 1988). Decontextualized learning is fostered when process is the content because procedural learning is more neutral, or context free. For example, steps to problem solving are quite easily mediated toward generalizations that transfer to varied contexts: Solving a "tower problem" is a typical strategic problem-solving technique in which an analogous situation is recognized and the solution mitigated according to previously learned procedures.

Crystallized Learning: Diamonds Are Forever

When process instruction becomes the content of instruction, transfer is enhanced because learning is crystallized. It is understood, as previously discussed, that skills, operations, and dispositions are taught through the vehicle of subject matter content. Students think well, with skill and grace and rigor, when they have something to think about; they work collaboratively and exemplify team skills when they are engaged in a project that requires cooperation; and they organize information when they have an abundance of data to manipulate. Thus, if students work with the subject matter content in wholesome, project-oriented instruction, in which these very processes are the focus and transfer of learning, all learning is crystallized. Not only is content learning enhanced and deepened, but the processes, skills, operations, and dispositions are, in turn, crystallized (Ben-Hur, 1994a).

In essence, understanding is deepened as students induce learning from specific situations and subsequently apply it and use it in other situations. For example, as students are immersed in a problem-based learning scenario concerning Columbus's voyage and the near mutiny on board, they use skills of analysis, conflict resolution, responsibility, and leadership, as well as generate ideas. Also, they learn about the historic moments, the concept of exploration, and the implications of the event. Not only do they gain insight into the knowledge base of the subject matter under scrutiny, but also they gain insight into the processes that undergird the learning of that knowledge base.

The crystallization of ideas elaborates, or "fattens," the ideas, and, at the same time, the crystallization process distills or "narrows" the learning until it is "crystal clear." Process instruction provides an opportunity for this crystallization to occur both in the use of skills, operations, and dispositions and in the extrapolation of the knowledge base itself.

Recontextualized Learning: When Am I Ever Gonna Use This?

Recontextualizing learning involves moving learning from one context to a new context. When process instruction becomes the content, transfer is enhanced as the skills, operations, and dispositions become portable as they are carried from one situation to the next and as they are recontextualized into meaningful application and use.

Recontextualized learning often requires mediation toward future applications (Feuerstein et al., 1980). Recontextualization, however, once realized, prolongs episodic learning; it generates relevant connections and ensures the longevity of learning. Recontextualized learning is a necessary step in transfer. It is the moment of meaning that occurs as the learners intentionally or unintentionally use skills, operations, and dispositions in similar or novel contexts.

One example of recontextualizing learning involves mindful abstraction, or bridging, of learning (Perkins & Salomon, 1988). A group of middle school students are expected to use "argument and evidence" to write a persuasive speech. The content of the argument, open to personal choice, encompasses issues of politics, economics, human rights, and the environment. Although the content of each speech is certainly one focus of importance, the process of arguing and providing evidence to support the argument is another critical focus of learning.

Although the content of the arguments may have transfer power, argument and evidence as an analysis technique is a highly portable process. Argument and evidence moves easily to proofs in math, to hypotheses and conclusions in science, to court cases in government class, and even to artistic criticism in literature class. Argument and evidence is recontextualized in each. Although the recontextualization of argument and evidence may require some mediation to move from science to math to literature, the process appears to have universal qualities that expedite transfer through recontextualization. In summary, recontextualized learning guarantees that the learning lives on— that it survives in other forms, tailored to the new context.

Energized Learning: Beyond Pour and Store

Process instruction enhances transfer because it fights the inert knowledge syndrome; it shifts from the pour-and-store model of learning the facts, data, and information of subject matter content to the dynamics of process instruction itself. It shifts toward the fluid use of skills, the management of operations, and the fueling of dispositions as students use, apply, and transfer these behaviors to varied and relevant situations.

Energized learning moves learners from the "nobody taught me" refrain to the idea that they are the "generation of information and thereby can be engaged in the processes of discovery and creativity" (Ben-Hur, 1994a, p. 30). Energized learning is epitomized in process instruction because the how is highlighted, rather than (or along with) the what. Students are led into active engagement in the steps and procedures of accomplishing something, rather than merely knowing of that something's existence. Inert knowledge, passive learners, and docile thinkers are instructional concerns that seem to disappear when process becomes content and is energized with action (Bransford, Sherwood, Vye, & Riser, 1986). For example, process instruction energizes learning even in the simplest of illustrations. Reading a chart of information and memorizing it for later recall form inert knowledge. Taking a survey, analyzing the results, and charting the data, on the other hand, constitute energized learning. The first scenario dictates passive learning, whereas the second creates active involved learning; one is content focused, the other is process focused.

When learning about coins in a process-oriented manner, youngsters are involved in using them to purchase items in their classroom store. Not only are the students cognizant of the value of the coins and why

SkyLight Training and Publishing, Inc.

they are used, but also they are immersed in a simulation of appropriate use. Students are immersed in sets of skills and various operations—problem solving and decision making—as well as the employment of the dispositions of efficacy and interdependence. The dynamics of interaction become as important as the content of the interaction. Learning is fluid and flexible and changing. It is activated and energized with vigor. Process instruction lends power to learning because students use their capacities for action and involvement.

When process instruction energizes the learning into powerful, dynamic, and ever changing ideas, transfer is, in turn, enhanced. Once learning is in motion, it moves easily from one situation to the next. Process instruction, by its very nature, is mobile; it moves skills, operations, and dispositions into diverse circumstances. In summary, process instruction is energized learning, and energized learning is portable, transferred learning.

Personalized Learning: Gotcha!

Process instruction enhances transfer because it personalizes learning. As the focus shifts toward skills, operations, and dispositions as content, students grasp the universal aspects and at the same time adapt the processes to a personal style. For example, while students learn a generic methodology for problem solving, each develops a set of procedures particular to his or her own problem solving. One student may examine both sides by comparing and contrasting ideas, whereas another may prefer to gather multiple solutions before analyzing any of them.

Personalization is simply the way to fingerprint the technique or series of techniques that seem to work best for each individual. It is the unending tailoring necessary for students seeking the perfect fit for productivity and progress in their own endeavors. The personalization process is critical to the enhancement of transfer because it helps learners internalize learning in deeply significant and personally relevant ways.

The personalization process builds individuals' capacities not only for relevant, immediate transfer but also for long-term use. This allows learners to tap into their resource banks throughout their lives. Learners are better able to recall and initiate appropriate behaviors if and when they are tagged with a personal reference point or telling label.

The skill of prediction may be labeled by some persons in their repertoire of strategies as "guessing" or "intuiting" outcomes on the basis of gut feelings. Others may refer to the same microskill of prediction as "forecasting" and rely in personal ways on the analysis of information to make predictions. Although differences between the two are subtle, they do, however, suggest the powerful role of personalization in the transfer process.

Process instruction, when more fully personalized, moves from tacit, implicit behaviors to aware, explicit actions. The tailoring process fosters metacognition (Brown, 1978). By understanding one's personal interpretation of craftsmanship as a feeling of pride in the completed task, the individual is more likely to explicitly transfer that disposition to multiple situations in life. For example, pride in craftsmanship may occur early in life. An individual may create a model airplane and have craftsmanship reappear later in a more abstract form of pride in a well-crafted argument. (Fogarty in Costa and Liebmann 1997)

In summary, process instruction enhances transfer by decontextualizing learning through generalizations, crystallizing learning with deepening under-standing, recontextualizing learning through meaningful applications, energiz-ing learning through active involvement, and personalizing learning through adaptations and tailoring.

When teachers ask, "What will students need to know and be able to do twenty-five years from now?" teachers are asking what learning needs to transfer into the students' adult lives. Students will need to know how to think, how to get along with others, how to solve problems, and how to make mindful decisions. At the same time, it seems that learning about learning, adopting a posture of inquiry, and acquiring a sense of efficacy are also desir-able goals for learners. To achieve those goals, we must push learners to the edge:

> Come to the edge, he said.
> They said: We are afraid.
> Come to the edge, he said.
> They came
> He pushed them . . . and they flew.
>> (Guillaume Apollinaire,
>> cited in Ferguson, 1980)

Brainworks
(ACTIVITIES)

TRANSFER TALES

In groups of three, use the jigsaw strategy (see chapter 5). Assign each person in the group two levels of transfer (see Figure 6.8).

Person #1: Level 1 and 2 (Ollie Overlooks; Dan Duplicates)
Person #2: Level 3 and 4 (Laura Replicates; Jonathan Integrates)
Person #3: Level 5 and 6 (Cathy Maps; Samantha Innovates)

Tell each person in the group to decide on the important features of his or her birds and to think of personal stories of transfer (transfer tales) to illustrate each of the two birds. Then, let them share in a teaching round so all three are informed about the six levels.

Brainstorms
(APPLICATION)

Create a list of possible reflection strategies and appropriate times to use those strategies.

Braindrain
(REFLECTION)

Reflect on reflection with the see saw graphic (see chapter 5), balancing the "Yes, buts" with "What ifs."

208

Brainwave
(THEME)

Assessment

There are those who believe in the saying Assessment drives instruction. While that may not be the whole story, there is a lot of truth to the familiar saying. In this age of standards and accountability, teachers and students are feeling the pressure. In fact, the schools are inundated with assessments and evaluations of all types.

This discussion covers the gamut of assessment strategies from traditional measures such as tests, report cards, and conferences to the more dynamic assessments that utilize student portfolios and performance tasks with scoring rubrics. The reasoned voice advocates a balance in the assessment process, with traditional, portfolio, and performance assessments all playing a role in creating the complete picture of student growth and progress. All these assessment strategies must focus on self-assessing components. While dynamic assessments appear more metacognitive, traditional assessments can easily be adapted to include a self-reflective element.

Brainwise
(STATEMENTS)

It may be that there is something going on in the brain that we don't have an inkling of at the moment.

Your brain is smarter than you are.

Instinct is what makes a genius a genius.

Braindrops
(STRATEGIES)

Assessment issues abound in the educational arena. Yet, a clear solution to the dilemma of how to assess student learning seems to be captured in the word "balance." When assessment practices are balanced across the spectrum of strategies, a full and comprehensive picture emerges about the student. Therefore, this discussion fosters a balance between traditional measures and more dynamic methods of assessment. The techniques range from traditional grades and report cards to student portfolios, performance assessments, and other dynamic ways to look at the total student.

In the brain-compatible classroom, self-reflection (thinking about one's thinking) and learning are expectations of all students. When students take charge of their own learning, they cannot help but be self-evaluative. By nature, learners want to know how they're doing. In the brain-compatible classroom, there are multiple ways for them to know how they're doing, including both traditional and dynamic assessments.

Student Assessment

Traditional Assessments

- Tests
  - Teacher Made
  - Criterion Referenced
  - Norm Referenced
- Grades
- Report Cards
- Parent Conferences

Dynamic Assessments

- Portfolio
- Performance

Figure 6.11

Traditional Assessment

Traditional assessments are familiar tools. These include many of the tried and true ways of evaluating student progress. In fact, quizzes, tests, grades, report cards, and parent conferences comprise those age-old means of assessing students.

TESTS

Tests have weathered the "test of time." They are embedded in everything we do in the school settings. There are the regular, run-of-the-mill quizzes and teacher-made tests that are used on weekly and sometimes on a daily basis that are used to motivate students to learn by keeping them accountable.

Then, there are the criterion-referenced tests published by the textbook companies. Of course, the states and/or the provinces have gotten into the

testing game and produce their own versions of criterion-referenced tests based on predetermined goals, aims, and objectives. Again, these can serve a purpose in terms of indicators of district strengths and weaknesses in programs and curricula, but often they are not great indicators of individual student learning because of the many uncontrollable variables.

And, then there are also the norm-referenced tests or standardized tests that are developed by national testing services and given widely across the states. These give a comparison that is believed to be fair, constant, and reliable. The benefit of the standardized tests and the information they provide is in the form of demographic data for national and international comparisons. However, when these scores are used as gatekeepers to various opportunities for students, their value diminishes; they are not always the best predictors of future successes.

Tests have a place in the overall assessment scheme. They do provide one form of feedback; however, their stature must not overshadow more dynamic forms of student evaluation.

GRADES

In addition to the multitude of tests, traditional assessment includes assigning students grades. The grades are either letter grades (A, B, C, D, or F), or they reflect numerical values such as 88 percent, 96 percent, and so on. Grades are given on daily work, homework, quizzes, and tests and for in-class participation. While they are considered objective measures, often they are actually subjectively based on individual teacher standards.

Yet, grades can be catalysts for learning—learners crave feedback from others. However, to make the grades meaningful motivators for learning, the students must become integral partners in the process. They must understand the standards and requirements and accept responsibility for attaining and achieving them.

REPORT CARDS

Report cards vary from check list to letter grades to anecdotal comments, and they often have detrimental effects on learning. They are summative records, showing the results, but not the process. While parents like the report card as a form for communicating how their children are doing in school, report cards alone, tell only part of the assessment picture.

PARENT CONFERENCES

Parent conferences often complement the report card and are usually held once a year in the fall. More often than not, they are one way communications by the teacher. However, there are teachers who include the student in the conference and foster conversation and input from the parents. Often, they provide insight into the dynamics of the family.

Dynamic Assessments

Dynamic assessments as opposed to traditional assessments employ the multiple intelligences approach and incorporate student portfolios and student performances in the repertoire of assessment strategies. In the brain-compatible classroom, student portfolios provide viable tools for self-reflection, while performances put the responsibility on the learner to actually perform the task and to demonstrate the learning. Assessment, as instruction, is brain-friendly. Therefore, students whose brains function best visually or kinesthetically are able to use these means rather than the usual verbal or mathematical measures.

PORTFOLIO

Student portfolios are selected collections of student work that demonstrate the growth and progress toward certain predetermined goals. The portfolio process, in its most basic form, includes a series of stages often referred to as collection, selection, and reflection. In each of these phases, the student takes the lead in the process because the real essence of the portfolio process is in the self-evaluation it promotes.

The collection of artifacts usually occurs over time and the students gather items in what is called a working portfolio. The portfolios are managed by the students, but the teacher may require certain items to be included for the final selection process.

Periodically, the collected items are inventoried and sorted. Usually, this selection process is accompanied by the reflection process. As students decide to keep an item for the "showcase" portfolio, or the final portfolio, they take time to write reflections, justifying why they have selected particular items.

The ultimate stage in the portfolio process is including it in the parent conference. In this way, the conference becomes a three-way conference with the teacher, the student, and the parent, each having a vital role. The portfolio emphasizes the growth and development of the student, while the report card offers a look at grades and rankings.

PERFORMANCE

Balancing the traditional measures and the portfolio process in the assessment repertoire is the strategy of performance assessments. In the performance task, students demonstrate what they have learned through a performance of some sort. These range form doing a lab experiment to giving a speech to executing an intricate routine in gymnastics class.

To incorporate the performance assessment into a full repertoire of assessments, the students must be informed of the standard expected for each performance. Once the standard is clear, criteria are delineated and indicators of meeting the criteria are explicitly described.

The scoring guide for the performance task is called a scoring rubric. It is, in essence, a chart or diagram that depicts the standards, the criteria, the indicators, and the points assigned to each.

The performance tasks add the elements of relevance and transfer to the assessment picture. They are needed additions if the assessment strategies are to be balanced for the best and most holistic picture of the student.

Brainworks
(ACTIVITIES)

FOLK PORTFOLIO

To develop the concept of student portfolios, the following exercise is suggested. Make the statement: An owl pellet is a portfolio. Then elicit reactions about the idea of the "collection" of artifacts the owl has eaten and regurgitated as a "folk portfolio." In small groups, generate lists of suggestions for other "folk portfolios." The ideas range from hope chests and jewelry boxes to the trunk of a car, a tool chest, and even the refrigerator door.

After the lists are completed and sampled, instruct the groups to list the characteristics or elements that these folk portfolios have in common. What is it that makes them portfolios?

After thinking about the attributes of a portfolio, have the groups synthesize their ideas into a definition of a portfolio. Read the definitions and discuss. Then, if time permits, show some student portfolios to illustrate how they have the same characteristics of the folk portfolios.

Brainstorms
(APPLICATION)

Create a riotous rubric activity as illustrated in Figure 6.12 around a fun topic to experience creating parallel structures. Then try a more serious rubric targeting an academic topic as depicted in Figure 6.13.

Braindrain
(REFLECTION)

Reflect on the assessment section using the tri pie (see Figure 6.14). In this graphic, compare three types of assessment: traditional, portfolio, performance.

RIOTOUS RUBRIC

Standard:

Criteria / Performance				

- -

Romance

Standard: Adventurous, mysterious, encounter with ambience and romatic setting.

	1	2	3	4
Secrecy Intrigue Mystery	All Know	Friends Know	Best Friend Knows	Only the Two of us Know
Adventure	Comatose at Home	Theme Park	Weekend Getaway	Paris
Ambience	T.V. Dinner at Kitchen Table	Fast Food	Candlelight Dinner	Cruise
Setting	Later After the Game	Same Time Next Year	Lunch Date	Midnight Rendezvous

Figure 6.12

SkyLight Training and Publishing, Inc.

ACADEMIC RUBRIC

Standard:

Performance \ Criteria				

- -

Integrated Curriculum

Standard: Rich, connected unit of study with rigor.

	1	2	3
RICHNESS (Multidimensional)	Contrived to fit across intelligences	Singular dimension	Breadth and depth across intelligences
RELATEDNESS (Connectedness)	No obvious connections across disciplines	Superficial connections across disciplines	Natural, genuine connections across disciplines
RIGOR (Higher-Order Thinking)	Pour and store, recall and regurgitate	Challenge: follow rigorous procedure	Struggle: getting stuck and getting unstuck

Figure 6.13

THE TRI PIE
Yes! No! Maybe So!

Issue

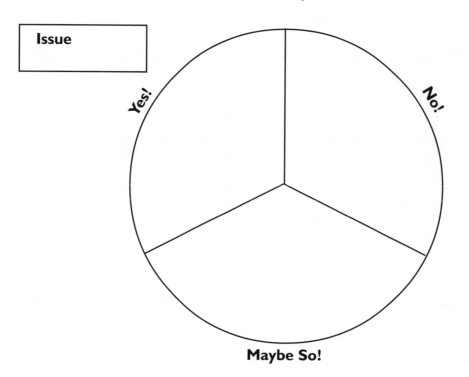

Maybe So!

Give the pros and cons of an issue, as well as a neutral position.

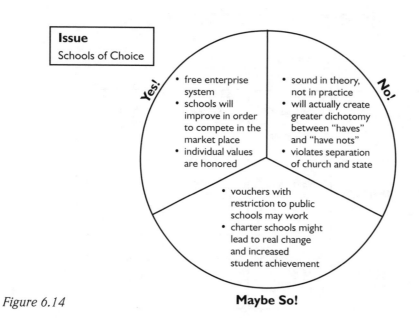

Issue

Schools of Choice

Yes!
- free enterprise system
- schools will improve in order to compete in the market place
- individual values are honored

No!
- sound in theory, not in practice
- will actually create greater dichotomy between "haves" and "have nots"
- violates separation of church and state

- vouchers with restriction to public schools may work
- charter schools might lead to real change and increased student achievement

Maybe So!

Figure 6.14

CHAPTER 7

TEACHER EVALUATION

The mediocre teacher tells. The good teacher explains. The superior teacher demonstrates. The great teacher inspires.

—WILLIAM ARTHUR WARD

CHAPTER 7

TEACHER EVALUATION

Evaluation Tool

The four-corner framework is one way of depicting the essential elements of a brain-compatible classroom (see Figure 7.1). Further, the four-corner framework provides an evaluation tool for analyzing the process called teaching. In fact, in its broadest sense, the framework provides a look at critical indicators for setting the highest standards for the teaching profession. It is, in essence, one way to evaluate the teaching performance evidenced by the learning environment and the resulting student achievement.

There is a direct connection between the learning environment and the learning outcomes. Only the teacher can truly determine if the learning environment is conducive to high expectations for all students to grow and learn, for all students to be equipped with the skills of life, for all students to be thoroughly engaged in the learning experience, and for all students to understand how to use the learning in relevant life situations.

The discussion that follows emphasizes the four-corner framework as one option for preparing a more formal teacher evaluation. The framework is a guide suggesting the research-based elements that impact on today's classroom. Within this broad framework, there is great flexibility in determining how the elements are creatively implemented and managed in the various classrooms. There are as many manifestations of these elements as there are creative teachers.

Essentially, the four-corner framework provides a complex taxonomy, rather than a hierarchy, of teaching performance. A look at the framework offers a better understanding of this complex structure.

FOUR-CORNER FRAMEWORK FOR THE BRAIN-COMPATIBLE CLASSROOM

Teaching FOR Thinking: Setting the Climate	**Teaching OF Thinking: Skills**
Emotions Enriched Environment	Types of Skills Development of Skills
Teaching WITH Thinking: Structuring Interaction	**Teaching ABOUT Thinking: Metacognition**
Active Learning Experiential Learning	Reflection Assessment

Figure 7.1

TEACHING PERFORMANCE

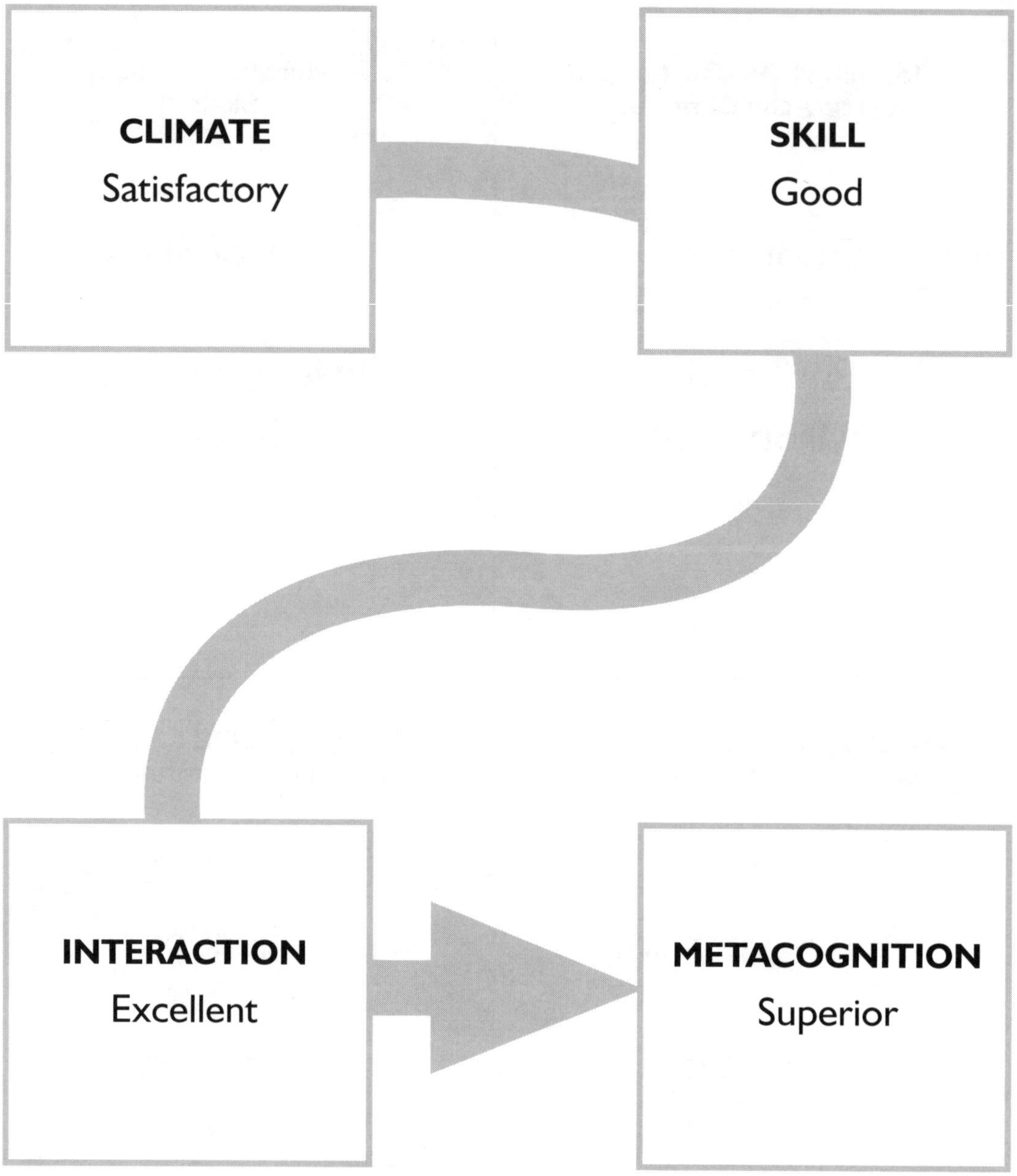

CLIMATE
Satisfactory

SKILL
Good

INTERACTION
Excellent

METACOGNITION
Superior

Figure 7.2

SkyLight Training and Publishing, Inc.

Moving from climate to skills to interaction to metacognition, as the backward "s" arrow indicates (see Figure 7.2), the satisfactory performance only moves to the level of good by including the elements of the satisfactory level. In other words, a performance is not evaluated as good if the teacher includes the skill elements without bringing in the climate pieces.

Each element is critical and is intricately combined in skillful teaching. The safe enriched classroom suggests a satisfactory level because the stimuli are there for learning. But when that climate is enhanced with direct instruction of skills, the level is raised to good. In turn, by immersing students in interactive learning the teacher moves the level of teaching to excellent because of what is known about active learning. And finally, the superior rating is attached to teaching that elicits student ownership and reflection. Figure 7.3 illustrates the taxonomy concept of the four-corner framework as an evaluation tool for teaching performance.

Four-Corner Taxonomy of Teaching Performance

Climate = Satisfactory
Climate + Skill = Good
Climate + Skill + Interaction = Excellent
Climate + Skill + Interaction + Metacognition = Superior

Figure 7.3

Now, knowing the taxonomy concept as applied to the framework (see Figure 7.4), each of the four elements are examined in greater detail. Exactly what does it look like and sound like to have a safe and caring climate and a rich environment; a repertoire of skills that are developing appropriately; opportunities for authentic, experiential learning—reflective learning that pushes transfer to relevant application? And, how do all these elements relate to standards of teaching?

Four-Corner Framework

SATISFACTORY	**GOOD**
Emotions	Types of Skills
Enriched Environment	Development of Skills
EXCELLENT	**SUPERIOR**
Active Learning	Reflection
Experiential Learning	Assessment

Figure 7.4

SETTING THE CLIMATE:
Teacher Evaluation=Satisfactory

When the teacher sets a caring climate, there is evidence that students feel a sense of trust, and risk-taking is the norm. Students question, they experiment, and they mess up, but in the safety of the classroom, they know it is okay to make mistakes, try again, and do things over. Student understanding and acceptance of the trial-and-error learning process is clearly the expectation of all.

In terms of environments that are stimuli-rich, the classroom is dripping with papers and posters in a visually enriched way; learning materials are plentiful and accessible and the learning environments are varied through creative use of furniture and fixtures. In this enriched learning environment, time is provided for exploration and discovery, and the learner-centered environment takes precedence over custodial and management concerns, yet the environment is obviously safe for the students to use creatively.

This teacher understands that with a classroom that is stimuli-rich and within a climate that is warm and caring, students will learn. They will explore, investigate, and think.

TEACHING THE SKILLS:
Teacher Evaluation=Good

By utilizing that safe, caring climate and the stimuli-rich environment as a backdrop, the next level of teaching performance includes explicit goals and direct instruction of skills that support those goals. The brain-compatible classroom caters to different types of skills, such as thinking skills, collaboration skills, technology skills, and performance skills, and to the guided development of those skills.

In this arena, the skillful teacher explicitly targets the skills of life, instructs students in the proper use of the skills and ensures the embedded use of the skills in appropriate applications. The teacher is aware of the developmental path from novice to expert and skillfully coaches the students as they progress through the various stages.

This teacher understands that while students are naturally curious and that learning is innate, skillful instruction is needed to guide and facilitate learning. The teacher in this classroom understands the role teaching plays in the learning process.

STRUCTURING INTERACTION:
Teacher Evaluation=Excellent

Within the caring climate of a sensory enriched classroom and as an integral part of the skill development, the exemplary classroom is a learner-centered classroom. It is a classroom of active learners, of experiential curriculum, and of engaged learning. The brain-compatible classroom is filled with the sounds and senses of discovery learning, hands-on activities, and cooperative structures. In the brain-friendly classroom, multidimensional models tap into the many intelligences of the students, and their intense involvement is recognized as that of a truly engaged learner. This classroom abounds with movement, murmurs, and visual and auditory evidence that the dendrites are growing.

This teacher goes beyond good direct instruction techniques and folds in the elements of interaction and active learning. The classroom in which students become intensely involved is the ultimate constructivist model.

TEACHING ABOUT THINKING:
Teacher Evaluation=Superior

The classrooms that evidence superior performances enhance the rich, safe climate, the skill development, and the active engaged learning scenario in a critical area. The brain-compatible classroom of superior quality adds the critical and obvious elements of student reflection and self-assessment as part of the norm. In this classroom, learning is shepherded and explicitly bridged across disciplines and into relevant life situations. The learning is guided by the teacher and the mediation is directly related to the desired results. Students do not learn inert knowledge, but rather, work to apply the knowledge in purposeful ways.

In addition, students in the superior quality classroom use brain-friendly strategies to help them to metacognitively plan, monitor, and evaluate their own progress. Students are grounded in the use of portfolios and performance learning tasks. They take ownership of their learning, are self-directed and self-assessing. In these classrooms, the students are in charge of their learning and it is obvious by their self-initiating ways.

This teacher transcends the science of teaching by incorporating climate, skill, and interaction issues and by understanding that learning is internalized through thoughtful reflection. This teacher values student mindfulness and fosters personalization of learning.

Brain-compatible classrooms are win-win situations: They enhance student learning as well as teaching practices. Figure 7.5 reiterates some of the ways teachers can start moving their teaching practices from satisfactory to superior, and thus improve the quality of their students' learning.

SkyLight Training and Publishing, Inc.

BRAIN-COMPATIBLE CLASSROOMS: IMPLICATIONS FOR TEACHING AND LEARNING

Setting the Climate FOR Thinking

- Nonverbal Signals
- DOVE Guidelines
- Emotional Intelligence
- Moral Intelligence
- Three-Story Intellect
- Fat/Skinny Questions
- People Search
- Wait-Time
- Response Strategies
- Socratic Dialogue
- Student Groupings
- Blocks of Time
- Year-Round Schools
- Room Arrangement
- Sensory Input
- Language Stimulation
- Learning Centers

Teaching the Skills OF Thinking

- Collaborative
- Thinking
- Technological
- Performance
- Problem-Solving
- Decision-Making
- Communication
- Research
- Word Processing
- Direct Instruction
- Developmental Path
- Embedded Application
- Peak Performance
- FLOW

Standards for High Achievement

Structuring the Interaction WITH Thinking

- Cooperative Structures
- Graphic Organizers
- Multiple Intelligences
  - Verbal/Linguistic
  - Logical/Mathematical
  - Bodily/Kinesthetic
  - Musical/Rhythmic
  - Visual/Spatial
  - Interpersonal
  - Intrapersonal
  - Naturalist
- Integrated Curriculum
  - Themes
  - Problem-Based Learning
  - Projects
  - Case Studies

Thinking ABOUT Thinking

- Personal Relevance
- Construct Knowledge
- Deep Understanding
- Generalizations
- Cognitive Mediation
- Metacognitive Reflection
- Application
- Transfer
- Traditional Assessment
- Portfolio Assessment
- Performance Assessment

Figure 7.5

APPENDIX A

SUGGESTED VIDEOS TO ILLUSTRATE THE FOUR-CORNER FRAMEWORK

SUGGESTED VIDEOS TO ILLUSTRATE THE FOUR-CORNER FRAMEWORK

Setting the Climate FOR Thinking	**Teaching the Skill OF Thinking**
To Sir With Love (High Expectations)	*Mr. Holland's Opus* (Skill Development)
Find the sequence in which the teacher sets the parameters for the classroom (by using the word *sir*) as a catalyst for a conversation about setting high expectations for all.	Find the part in which the teacher works with the young athlete to "feel the rhythm" for marching to begin a discussion on skill development.
Structuring Interaction WITH Thinking	**Teaching ABOUT Thinking**
Teacher (Experiential Learning)	*Dead Poets Society* (Reflection)
Find the segment in which the teacher simulates the "crossing of the Delaware by George Washington" to begin a discussion on experiential learning.	Find the part in which the teacher has the boys rip the books and then recites "What will your verse be?" Use it as a lead-in about "big ideas" to reflect on.

APPENDIX B

THE BRAIN

THE BRAIN

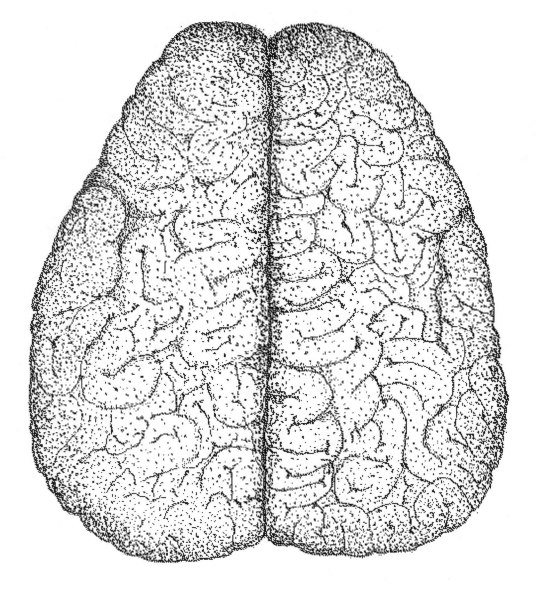

APPENDIX C

READING LIST

READING LIST

Brain-Based Learning, by Eric Jensen (Turning Point Publishing, 1996).

A Celebration of Neurons: An Educator's Guide to the Human Brain, by Robert Sylwester (ASCD, 1995).

Education on the Edge of Possibility, by Renate Nummela Caine and Geoffrey Caine (ASCD, 1997).

Emotional Intelligence: Why It Can Matter More Than IQ, by Daniel Goleman (Bantam Books, 1995).

The Growth of the Mind and the Endangered Origins of Intelligence, by Stanley I. Greenspan (Addison-Wesley, 1997).

Inside the Brain: Revolutionary Discoveries of How the Mind Works, by Ronald Kotulak (Andrews and McMeel, 1996).

Making Connections: Teaching and the Human Brain, by Renate Nummela Caine and Geoffrey Caine (Addison-Wesley, 1994).

Mindshifts: A Brain-Based Process for Restructuring Schools and Renewing Education, by Geoffrey Caine, Renate Nummela Caine and Sam Crowell (Zephyr Press, 1994).

Outsmarting IQ: The Emerging Science of Learnable Intelligence, by David Perkins (Free Press, 1995).

GLOSSARY

GLOSSARY

Amygdala: the almond-shaped structure in the brain's limbic system that encodes emotional messages to long-term storage

Axon: the neuron's long and unbranched fiber that carries impulses away from the cell to the next neuron

Bilateralization: two hemispheres of the brain working together

Binocular Vision: the ability to coordinate the images from both eyes

Brain Compatible: teaching/learning processes that parallel or complement the way the brain/mind makes meaning and remembers

Brain Stem: one of the three major parts of the brain; receives sensory input and monitors vital functions such as heartbeat, body temperature, and digestion

Cerebellum: one of the three major parts of the brain; coordinates muscle movement

Cerebrum: the largest of the three major parts of the brain; controls sensory interpretation, thinking, and memory

Chemical signal: neurotransmitters that create connection between neurons (brain cells)

Chunking: the ability of the brain to perceive a coherent group of items as a single item or a chunk

Closure: the time when the mind of the learner can summarize for itself its perception of what has been learned; when the teacher gives specific directions for what the learner should mentally process and provides adequate time to accomplish it; usually the last opportunity the learner has to attach sense and meaning to the new learning, both of which are critical requirements for retention

Clustering: free-flowing technique to plot spontaneous verbal associations; used in writing to initiate, focus, or elaborate

Cooperative Group: small structured group in which members have designated roles and responsibilities

Cooperative Structure: interactive strategies used in small collaborative group work

Corpus Callosum: the bridge of nerve fibers that connect the left and right cerebral hemispheres, allowing communication between them

Critical Thinking: using skills of analysis and evaluation to determine the worth of an idea; critiquing

Decision Making: judging choices and basing final selection on evaluation of criteria

Deductive Reasoning: reasoning from a general rule to a specific case (i.e., Does it fit the rule or generalization?)

Dendrite: the branched extension from the cell body of a neuron that receives impulses from nearby neurons through synaptic contacts

Direct Instruction Model: Madeline Hunter's model of teaching that involves seven steps: an anticipatory set, a clear objective, instructor input, guided practice, feedback, independent application, and evaluation

DOVE Guidelines: guidelines to promote an open, nonjudgmental environment for group sharing; an acronym representing the following: Defer judgment, Opt for original ideas, Vast number is needed, Expand by piggybacking on others' ideas

Electrical Impulse: activity inside the brain cell caused by a nerve impulse or sensory input of some sort

Embedded Application: use of a skill within a specific context (e.g., applying the skill of keyboarding during a word-processing activity)

Emotional Intelligence: ability to function effectively in the "affective domain"

FLOW: state of immersed activity that creates a sense of harmony and effortlessness as defined by Csikszentmihalyi (1990)

Four-Corner Framework: teaching *for, of, with,* and *about* thinking

Glial Cells: special "glue" cells in the brain that surround each neuron providing support, protection, and nourishment

Graphic Organizer: visual format used to organize ideas, concepts, and information; also called visual organizer

Hemisphericity: the notion that the two cerebral hemispheres are specialized and process information differently

Hippocampus: a brain structure that compares new learning to past learning and encodes information from working memory to long-term storage

Journal: a student diary consisting of verbal and visual entries, usually including personal reflections, self-assessments, and spontaneous writing

Left Hemisphere: the *logical* hemisphere that monitors the areas for speech, reading, and writing; analyzes and evaluates factual material in a rational way; understands the literal interpretation of words; detects time and sequence; recognizes words, letters, and numbers

Limbic System: the structures at the base of the cerebrum that control emotions

Log: a student record consisting of verbal and visual entries reflecting personal reactions to learning, usually in relation to a specific course or topic

Macroskill: critical and creative processes comprised of several microskills (e.g., synthesis requires skills of analytic evaluation and divergent thinking)

Metacognitive Processing: thinking about thinking; tracking how one thinks, using structured discussion or written records

Microskill: skill taught in isolation (e.g., classifying, sequencing, comparing and contrasting)

Moral Intelligence: ability to know one's way around; to act with wisdom and finesse

Mrs. Potter's Questions: four questions used to assess students' learning and performance: What was I expected to do? What did I do well? If I did the same task again, what would I do differently? What help do I need?

Multiple Intelligences: eight intelligences, as defined by Howard Gardner

Verbal/Linguistic Intelligence: the ability to use with clarity the core operations of language

Musical/Rhythmic Intelligence: the ability to use the core set of musical elements

Logical/Mathematical Intelligence: the ability to use inductive and deductive reasoning, solve abstract problems, and understand complex relationships

Interpersonal Intelligence: the ability to get along with, interact with, work with, and motivate others toward a common goal

Visual/Spatial Intelligence: the ability to perceive the visual world accurately and to be able to recreate one's visual experiences graphically

Intrapersonal Intelligence: the ability to form an accurate model of oneself and to use that model to operate effectively in life

Bodily/Kinesthetic Intelligence: the ability to control and interpret body motions, manipulate physical objects, and establish harmony between the body and mind

Naturalist Intelligence: the ability to see similarities and differences in one's environment and to understand the interrelationships of the ecosystem

Myelin: a fatty substance that surrounds and insulates a neuron's axon

Neocortex: the outer layer of the brain; located just below the skull and pertaining to the cerebrum or thinking brain

Neural Network, or pattern: a connection among neurons that forms a schema or pathway, which is strengthened through frequent use

Neural Plasticity: ability of the brain to wire and rewire itself by making and breaking connections between neurons

Neuron: the basic cell making up the brain and nervous system; consists of a long fiber called an axon, which transmits impulses, and many shorter fibers called dendrites, which receive the impulses

Neurotransmitter: one of over fifty chemicals stored in axon sacs; transmits impulses from neuron to neuron across the synaptic gap

Peak Performance: the expert performance or elegant solution

Portfolio: collection of student work, usually comprised of a student's best work or work that shows development; also used to collect a group's or class's work

Problem Solving: specific strategies that use creative synthesis and critical analysis to generate viable alternatives to perplexing situations

Purpose: a statement defining *why* students should accomplish the learning objective (Whenever possible, it should refer to how the new learning is related to prior and future learnings to facilitate positive transfer and meaning.)

Reflection: the result of thoughts, ideas, or conclusions expressed in words (written or verbal); responses to thoughtful interludes

Right Hemisphere: the *intuitive* hemisphere; gathers information more from images than words; looks for patterns and can process many kinds of information simultaneously; interprets language through context-body language and tone of voice, rather than through literal meanings; specializes in spatial perception and is capable of fantasy and creativity; recognizes places, faces, and objects

Rubric: assessment tool that specifies criteria for different levels of performance

Self-Assessment: any tool or strategy used by an individual to examine and evaluate one's own work

Standard: criterion used to assess performance

Synapse: the microscopic gap between the axon of one neuron and the dendrite of another

Three-Story Intellect Verbs, or Questions: categorization of verbs to use in formulating questions that elicit responses based on different levels of thinking: one-story verbs prompt factual recall; two-story verbs ask for comparisons, reasoning, and generalizations; and three-story verbs stimulate imagination, hypotheses, and syntheses

Transfer: a principle of learning described as a two-part process (1) the effect that past learning has on the processing of new learning (2) the degree to which the new learning will be useful to the learner in the future

Triune Brain: an early model of the brain defined by MacLean as the three different phases of the evolution of the human brain: reptilian, paleomammalian, neomammalian (This model is now suspect; see chapter 1.)

REFERENCE
LIST

REFERENCE LIST

Adler, Mortimer J., and Charles van Doren. 1972. *How to read a book.* New York: Simon and Schuster.

Ainsworth-Land, Vaune, and N. Fletcher. 1979. *Making waves with creative problem solving.* Buffalo, NY: D.O.K.

American Educational Research Association. 1997a. *Expanding our concept of intelligence: What's missing and what could we gain?* Chicago, IL: AERA's Annual Meeting.

———. 1997b. *Neuroscience and education: What do we know about the brain that has implications for education? (2 tapes)* Chicago, IL: AERA's Annual Meeting.

Armstrong, Thomas. 1987. *In their own way.* Los Angeles, CA: J. P. Tarcher.

———. 1993. *Seven kinds of smart: Indentifying and developing your many intelligences.* New York: Penguin.

Aronson, Elliot, ed. 1978. *The jigsaw classroom.* Beverly Hills, CA: Sage Publications.

Association for Supervision and Curriculum Development. 1996. *The Brain, the mind, and the classroom (Audiotapes 1 and 2).* Alexandria, VA: ASCD.

———. 1997a. *A new vision for assessment: Matching assessment reforms with current brain research.* ASCD 52nd Annual Conference. Alexandria, VA: ASCD.

———. 1997b. *How should educators use new knowledge from brain research?* ASCD 52nd Annual Conference. Alexandria, VA: ASCD.

Baron, Joan B., and Robert J. Sternberg, eds. 1987. *Teaching thinking skills: Theory and practice.* New York: W. H. Freeman and Company.

Barrett, Susan L. 1992. *It's all in your head: A guide to understanding your brain and boosting your brain power.* Minneapolis, MN: Free Spirit Publishing.

Beane, James, ed. 1995. *Toward a coherent curriculum: 1995 yearbook of the ASCD.* Alexandria, VA: ASCD.

Bellanca, James. 1984a. *Quality circles for educators.* Arlington Heights, IL: IRI/SkyLight Training and Publishing.

————. 1984b. *Skills for critical thinking.* Arlington Heights, IL: IRI/SkyLight Training and Publishing.

Bellanca, James, and Robin Fogarty. 1986a. *Catch them thinking: A handbook of classroom strategies.* Arlington Heights, IL: IRI/SkyLight Training and Publishing.

————. 1986b. *Planning for thinking: A guidebook for instructional leaders.* Arlington Heights, IL: IRI/SkyLight Training and Publishing.

————. 1986c. *Teach them thinking.* Arlington Heights, IL: IRI/SkyLight Training and Publishing.

————. 1991. *Blueprints for thinking in the cooperative classroom.* Arlington Heights, IL: IRI/SkyLight Training and Publishing.

Ben-Hur, Meir, ed. 1994a. *On Feuerstein's Instrumental Enrichment: A Collection.* Arlington Heights, IL: IRI/SkyLight Training and Publishing.

————. 1994b. Thoughts on teaching and transfer. Paper presented at IRI/ SkyLight Consultant Conference, December, Chicago, IL.

Beyer, Barry K. 1983. Common sense about teaching thinking skills. *Educational Leadership* 41(3): 44–49.

————. 1984. Improving thinking skills—defining the problem. *Phi Delta Kappan* 65(7): 486–490.

————. 1985. Teaching thinking skills: How the principal can know they are being taught. *NASSP Bulletin* January.

————. 1987. *Practical strategies for the teaching of thinking.* Boston, MA: Allyn & Bacon.

Biondi, A., ed. 1972. *The creative process.* Buffalo, NY: D.O.K.

Black, H., and S. Black. 1981. *Figural analogies.* Pacific Grove, CA: Midwest Publications.

Bloom, Benjamin S. 1981. *All our children learning: A primer for parents, teachers, and educators.* New York: McGraw-Hill.

Bloom, B. S.; M. D. Engelhart; E. J. Furst; W. H. Hill; and D. R. Kratwohl. 1956. *Taxonomy of educational objectives: Cognitive domain, Handbook I.* New York: David McKay Co.

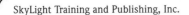

Bloom, Floyd E., and Arlyne Lazerson. 1988. *Brain, mind, and behavior.* 2nd Edition. New York: W. H. Freeman and Company.

Brandt, Ron. 1988. On teaching thinking: A conversation with Arthur Costa. *Educational Leadership* 45(7): 10–13.

Brandt, Ron, moderator. 1997. *How should educators use the new knowledge from the brain research?* ASCD 52nd Annual Conference. Alexandria, VA: ASCD.

Bransford, J.; R. Sherwood; N. Vye; and J. Riser. 1986. Teaching thinking and problem solving: Research foundations. *American Psychologist* 41(10): 1078–1089.

Brooks, J. G. and M. G. Brooks. 1993. *In search of understanding: The case for the constructivist classroom.* Alexandria, VA: ASCD.

Brown, A. L. 1978. Knowing when, where, and how to remember: A problem of metacognition. In *Advances in instructional psychology (Vol. 1),* edited by R. Glaser. Hillsdale, NJ: Lawrence Erlbaum Associates.

Bruner, Jerome S. 1973. Readiness for learning. In *Beyond the information given: Studies in the psychology of knowing,* edited by Jeremy Anglin. New York: Norton.

Bruner, Jerome S.; Jacqueline Goodnow; and George A. Austin. 1967. *A study of thinking.* New York: Wiley.

Burns, Marilyn. 1975. *I hate mathematics.* Boston, MA: Little, Brown and Co.

———. 1976. *The book of think or how to solve a problem twice your size.* Boston, MA: Little, Brown and Co.

Buscaglia, Leo F. 1972. *Love.* Thoroughfare, NJ: Slack.

Buzan, Tony. 1984. Make the most of your mind. New York: Linden Press/Simon & Schuster.

Caine, Geoffrey; Renate N. Caine; and Sam Crowell. 1994. *Mindshifts: A brain-based process for restructuring schools and renewing education.* Tucson, AZ: Zephyr Press.

Caine, Renate N., and Geoffrey Caine. 1991. *Making connections: Teaching and the human brain.* Alexandria, VA: ASCD.

————. 1997. *Education on the edge of possibility.* Alexandria, VA: ASCD.

Calvin, William H. 1996. *How brains think: Evolving intelligence, then and now.* New York: Basic Books.

Chapman, Carolyn. 1993. *If the shoe fits: How to develop multiple intelligences in the classroom.* Palatine, IL: IRI/SkyLight.

Coles, Robert. 1997. *The moral intelligence of children: How to raise a moral child.* New York: Random House.

College Board. 1983. *Academic preparation for college: What students need to know and be able to do.* New York: College Board.

Costa, Arthur. 1991. *The school as a home for the mind.* Arlington Heights, IL: IRI/SkyLight Training and Publishing.

Csikszentmihalyi, Mihaly. 1990. *Flow: The psychology of optimal experience.* New York: Harper & Row.

Damasio, Antonio R. 1994. *Descartes' error: Emotion, reason, and the human brain.* New York: Avon Books.

Davis, Joel. 1997. *Mapping the mind.* New York: Carol Publishing Group.

Dewey, J. 1938. *Experience and education.* New York: Collier.

Diamond, Marian. 1988. *Enriching heredity: The impact of the environment on the anatomy of the brain.* New York: Free Press.

Eisner, E. 1997. Cognition and Representation: A Way to Pursue the American Dream? *Phi Delta Kappan* 78(5) January: 348–353.

Epstein, H. 1978. *Education and the brain: The 77th yearbook of the national society for the study of education.* Chicago, IL: The Yearbook Committee and Associated Contributors, University of Chicago Press.

ESS Science Series. 1966. *Problem cards: Attribute games and problems.* New York: Webster Division of McGraw-Hill.

Ferguson, Marilyn. 1987. *The aquarian conspiracy: Personal and social transformation in the 1980s.* Los Angeles: J. P. Tarcher.

Feuerstein, Reuven. 1990. *Instrumental Enrichment.* Baltimore: University Park Press.

Feuerstein, R.; Y. Rand; M. B. Hoffman; and R. Miller. 1980. *Instrumental enrichment.* Baltimore: University Park Press.

Flavell, John H. 1979. Metacognitions and cognitive monitoring: A new area of child developmental inquiry. *Applied Psychology* 34: 906–911.

Fogarty, Robin. 1989. *From training to transfer: The role of creativity in the adult learner.* Unpublished doctoral dissertation, Loyola University of Chicago.

———. 1991. *The mindful school: How to integrate the curricula.* Arlington Heights, IL: IRI/SkyLight Training and Publishing.

———. 1994. *The mindful school: How to teach for metacognitive reflection.* Palatine, IL: IRI/SkyLight.

———. 1997. *Problem-based learning and other curriculum models for the multiple intelligences classroom.* Arlington Heights, IL: IRI/SkyLight Training and Publishing.

Fogarty, Robin, and James Bellanca. 1987. *Patterns for thinking, Patterns for transfer.* Palatine, IL: IRI/SkyLight.

Fogarty, Robin; David Perkins; and John Barell. 1992. *The mindful school: How to teach for transfer.* Palatine, IL: IRI/SkyLight.

Fogarty, Robin, and Sally Berman. 1997. *Project Learning for the multiple intelligences classroom.* Arlington Heights, IL: SkyLight Training and Publishing.

Fogarty, Robin, and Judy Stoehr. 1995. *Integrating curricula with multiple intelligences.* Arlington Heights, IL: IRI/SkyLight Training and Publishing.

Gagne, R. M. 1968. Learning hierarchies. *Educational Psychologist* 6: 1–9.

Gardner, Howard. 1983. *Frames of mind: The theory of multiple intelligences.* New York: Basic Books.

———. 1993. *Multiple intelligences: The theory in practice.* New York: HarperCollins.

Gibbs, Nancy. 1995. The EQ Factor. *Time* 146(14) October: 60 (8).

Glick, M. L., and K. J. Holyoak. 1987. The cognitive basis of knowledge transfer. In *Transfer of training,* eds., S. M. Cormier, and J. D. Hagman. San Diego, CA: Academic Press.

Goleman, Daniel. 1995a. *Emotional intelligences: Why it can matter more than IQ.* New York: Bantam Books.

————. 1995b. *Emotional intelligences: Why it can matter more than IQ (Audio Renaissance tapes).* Los Angeles, CA.

————. 1997. *Emotional intelligence: A new model for curriculum development (audiotape).* ASCD 52nd Annual Conference. Alexandria, VA: ASCD.

Gould, S. J. 1981. *The mismeasure of man.* New York: Norton.

Harmin, Merrill. 1994. *Inspiring active learning: A handbook for teachers.* Alexandria, VA: ASCD.

Hart, Leslie A. 1983. *Human brain human learning.* Kent, WA: Books for Educators.

Healy, Jane M. 1987. *Your child's growing mind: A guide to learning and brain development from birth to adolescence (A Main Street Book).* New York: Doubleday.

————. 1990. *Endangered minds.* New York: Touchstone.

Hemingway, Ernest. 1952. *The old man and the sea.* New York: Scribner.

Herrmann, Ned. 1988. *The creative brain.* Lake Lure, NC: The Ned Herrmann Group.

Howard, Pierce J. 1994. *The owner's manual for the brain: Everyday applications from the mind-brain research.* Austin, TX: A Bard Productions Book.

Hunter, Madeline. 1971. *Transfer.* El Segundo, CA: TIP.

————. 1982. *Teaching for transfer.* El Segundo, CA: TIP Publications.

Isaacson, Robert L. 1982. *Limbic system.* 2nd ed. New York: Plenum Press.

Jensen, Eric. 1988. *SuperTeaching: Master strategies for building student success.* Del Mar, CA: Turning Point for Teachers.

————. 1995. *The learning brain.* Del Mar, CA: Turning Point Publishing.

————. 1996a. *Brain-based learning.* Del Mar, CA: Turning Point Publishing.

————. 1996b. Brain research/learning. National Conference of Texas. Austin, TX: Reliable Communications.

————. 1996c. *Completing the puzzle: A brain-based approach to learning.* Del Mar, CA: Turning Point Publishing.

————. 1997a. *Brain-compatible strategies: Hundreds of easy-to-use brain-compatible activities that boost attention, motivation, learning and achievement.* Del Mar, CA: Turning Point Publishing.

————. 1997b. *Links between diversity training and brain research (audio- tape).* ASCD 52nd Annual Conference. Alexandria, VA: ASCD. (Chesapeake Audio/ Video Communications Inc.)

Johnson, David; Roger Johnson; and Edythe Johnson Holubec. 1986. *Circles of learning: Cooperation in the classroom.* Alexandria, VA: ASCD.

Johnson, Roger, and David Johnson. 1982. Cooperation in learning: Ignored but powerful. *Lyceum,* October.

Joyce, Bruce R. 1986. *Improving America's schools.* New York: Longman.

Joyce, Bruce R., and Beverly Showers. 1980. Improving inservice training: The message of research. *Educational Leadership* February: 380.

————. 1983. *Power in staff development through research and training.* Alexandria, Va: ASCD.

Karplus, R. 1974. *Science curriculum improvement study teachers handbook.* Berkeley, CA: University of California.

Kerman, Sam. 1979. Teacher Expectations and Student Achievement. *Phi Delta Kappa* 60(10) January 716–718.

Klein, Joe. 1997. Clintons on the brain: Will this be their legacy? Letter from Washington. *The New Yorker* 73(4) March 17: 59–63.

Kotulak, Ronald. 1996. *Inside the Brain.* Kansas, MO: Andrews and Mcmeel, A University Press Syndicate Company.

Kovalik, S. 1989. *Integrated Thematic Instruction (ITT).* Susan Kovalik & Assoc.

Krupp, J. A. 1981. Adult development. Connecticut, MA: Adult Development and Learning.

————. 1982. The adult learner. Connecticut, MA: Adult Development and Learning.

Lach, J. 1997. Your child's first steps: Turning on the motor. *Newsweek Special Edition: Your Child from Birth to Three* Spring/Summer: 26–27.

Larkin, J. H.; J. McDermott; D. P. Simon; and H. A. Simon. 1980. Expert and novice performance in solving physics problems. *Science* June 20: 1335–1342.

Lazear, David. 1991. *Seven ways of teaching.* Arlington Heights, IL: IRI/SkyLight Training and Publishing.

LeDoux, J. E. 1996. *The emotional brain: The mysterious underpinnings of emotional life.* New York: Simon & Schuster.

Luria, Aleksandr. 1976. *Working brain: An introduction to neuropsychology.* New York: Basic Books.

Lyman, F., and J. McTighe. 1988. Cueing thinking in the classroom: the promise of theroy-embedded tools. *Educational Leadership* 45(7) p. 18–24.

McCloskey, M.; A. Carmazza; and B. Green. 1980. Curvilinear motion in the absence of external forces: Naive beliefs about the motion of objects. *Science* December 5: 1139–1141.

Machado, Luis A. 1980. *The right to be intelligent.* New York: Pergamon Press.

MacLean, P. D. 1969. New trends in man's evolution. In A triune concept of the brain and behavior. Paper presented at Queen's University, Ontario, Ann Arbor, MI: Book on Demand, University Microfilms International.

———. 1978. A mind of three minds: Educating the triune brain. In *Education and the brain,* edited by Jeanne Chall and Allan Mirsky. Chicago, IL: Unviersity of Chicago Press.

Maraviglia, C. 1978. *Creative problem-solving think book.* Buffalo, NY: D.O.K.

Margulies, N. 1997. *Inside Brian's brain: Interactive comics, vol. 3.* Tucson, AZ: Zephyr Press.

Marzano, R. J., and D. E. Arredondo. 1986. Restructuring schools through the teaching of thinking skills. *Educational Leadership* 43(8) May: 20–26.

Nash, Madeline. 1997a. Addicted: Why do people get hooked? Mounting evidence points to a powerful brain chemical called dopamine. *Time* 149(18) May 5: 68 (7).

———. 1997b. Fertile Minds. *Time* 149(18) February 3: 48 (9).

Nickerson, Ray S. 1982. *Understanding Understanding.* BBN Report No. 5087.

————. 1983. Computer programming as a vehicle for teaching thinking skills. *Journal of Philosophy for Children* 4(3 & 4).

Nickerson, Ray S.; David N. Perkins; and Edward E. Smith. 1985. *Teaching thinking.* BBN Report No. 5575.

Nickerson, R. S.; W. S. Shepard; and J. Hermstein. 1984. *The teaching of learning strategies.* BBN Report No. 5578.

Nisbett, R., and L. Ross. 1980. *Human inference: Strategies and shortcomings of social judgment.* Englewood Cliffs, N.J.: Prentice-Hall.

Noller, Ruth. 1977. *Scratching the surface of creative problem solving: A bird's eye view of CPS.* Buffalo, NY: D.O.K.

Noller, R.; S. Parnes; and A. Biondi. 1976. *Creative action book.* New York: Charles Scribner & Sons.

Noller, R.; D. Treffinger; and E. Houseman. 1979. *It's a gas to be gifted: Scratching the surface: Creative problem solving in math.* Buffalo, NY: D.O.K.

Oakes, Jeannie, and Martin Lipton. 1993. Detracking schools: Early lessons from the field. In *The challenge of detracking: A collection*, edited by James Bellanca and Elizabeth Swartz. Arlington Heights, IL: IRI/SkyLight Training and Publishing.

Ogle, Donna. 1989. Implementing strategic teaching. *Educational Leadership* 46(4) December–January: 47–48, 57–60.

Orstein, Robert, and David Sobel. 1987. *The healing brain: Breakthrough discoveries about how the brain keeps us healthy.* New York: Simon and Schuster.

Osborn, A. F. 1963. *Applied imagination.* New York: Charles Scribner & Sons.

Palincsar, A. S., and A. Brown. 1984. Reciprocal teaching of comprehension-fostering and comprehension-monitoring activities. *Cognition and Instruction* 1(2): 117–175.

Parker, S. 1995. *Brain Surgery for Beginners and other major operations for minors.* Brookfield, CT: The Millbrook Press.

Parnes, Sidney. 1972. *Creativity: Unlocking human potential.* Buffalo, NY: D.O.K.

————. 1975. *Aha! Insights into creative behavior.* Buffalo, NY: D.O.K.